Diary of a
YANKEE-HATER

Diary of a
YANKEE-HATER

by Bob Marshall

Franklin Watts/*New York*/*London*/*Toronto*/*Sydney*/1981

Library of Congress Cataloging in Publication Data

Marshall, Bob.
Diary of a Yankee-hater.

1. New York (City). Baseball Club (American League)
—History. I. Title.
GV875.N4M37   796.357'64'097471   80-28635
ISBN 0-531-09945-8

Acknowledgments

Every baseball fan has memories, but in writing this book I found that mine were never as reliable as *The Baseball Encyclopedia*. I also owe a debt of thanks to the good friends who hosted my Yankee-hating excursions from New York, Jennie and Andy Gardner, Patty Moore and Bob Inderman and Manuele and Dick Wasserman; to those who helped me get a view of the ball field different than that from my customary seat in the upper deck, Bob Losey, Mary Gibbons, Jack Wasserman, Ed Spalty and Ted Emery; to those who commented on portions of the manuscript, Richard Marshall and Peter Sharpe; and, for her overall support, to Yvonne Vanterpool. Without the help of Philip Spitzer and Bob Levine, my agent and my editor, this diary would be reposing with the diary of my Peace Corps years and other private artifacts of my life.

From the day this journal was conceived until its completion, its biggest supporter has been my wife, Siri. For her patience and understanding while I spent hours in front of the television, for her willingness to pass up Italy for a summer vacation trip to Kansas City in the middle of a heat wave, and for her help on the manuscript itself, I will forever be grateful. Her encouragement never flagged, even though for one whole baseball season she had to be satisfied with the traditional refrain of the baseball fan, "Wait till next year."

To Dad

Diary of a
YANKEE-HATER

INTRODUCTION
The Sport of Yankee-Hating

Summer 1979. This book was born on July 27, 1979. That night, Cecil Cooper of the Milwaukee Brewers hit a two-out, two-strike home run off Goose Gossage in the bottom of the ninth inning to beat the New York Yankees, 6–5. It was Cooper's third home run of the game, and the 48,000 fans in Milwaukee's County Stadium went wild. Listening to a radio in New York, I went wild.

The excitement and happiness I felt the moment the ball left Cooper's bat and Yankee broadcaster Phil Rizzuto said "Uh-oh . . ." was an emotion I wanted to preserve, and if possible share. And I knew the audience with whom I wanted to share it. For while the Yankees may be the most popular team in baseball, there is another reason why they are the biggest gate attraction, year in and out, on the road as well as at home. Other teams may have more fanatical devotees, but no team arouses the negative passions the Yankees do. There are millions of fans who would rather have their home team beat the Yankees than anyone else in the league. And there are others who root not so much *for* some other team, but, simply and continually, *against* the Yankees. It is this combined legion of Yankee-haters that I am a part of. And it is for these Yankee-haters, whoever and wherever they may be, that I set out to document the New York Yankees' 1980 season.

Fall 1979. With the possible exceptions of my wife and my mother, everyone reading this book is undoubtedly familiar with the causes of Yankee-hating, and I will not belabor or attempt to analyze them in the pages that follow. The goal of this book instead is to follow one Yankee season from the Yankee-hater's perspective. The unknowns that lie ahead are the events of 1980; the point of view is a given. But in case somebody still asks, Where is it given? I offer five attributes of the New York Yankees, generic and specific, that Yankee-haters all over the country would agree on.

1. They win too much. America loves and roots for the underdog. The Yankees have not only won more pennants and World Series than any other team, their lead in this department is obscene: the Yankees have twenty-two World Championships in their collection, the runner-up St. Louis Cardinals have eight.

2. They win by buying the best players, and paying them too much. This started in 1920, when Colonel Ruppert bought Babe Ruth from the Red Sox, and has accelerated in the present free-agent era. Offering postseason dividends and commercial tie-ins, the Yankees have an edge in signing any player interested in money (did I leave anybody out?). And while other teams worry about disrupting their salary structure, the Yankees pay $125,000 to a utility infielder who bats one hundred times a year.

3. They get more attention than they deserve. The Yankees are in New York, which is not only the biggest city in the country but is the advertising and media capital of the world. If you want to have a candy bar named after you, someone once said, you have to play in New York.

4. They are arrogant, egotistical and loudmouthed. No doubt influenced by 1., 2. and 3., Yankee players seem more interested in their personal statistics and commercial endorsements than in the welfare of the team. How much playing time a player gets often seems more important than whether the team is winning, and the players are all quite ready to voice their personal feelings to the media mob swarming around them.

5. Their rightfielder is Reggie Jackson. Unquestionably the most controversial, and certainly not the best, baseball player in the game today, Reggie is the personification of items 1., 2., 3. and 4. Reggie is such an immature, attention-seeking prima donna, and still such a relative newcomer to the Yankee family, that it is possible to hate Reggie and not be a Yankee-hater. But for all those who are in the opposition party to begin with, Reggie is the icing on the cake.

Chapter 1
A NEW TEAM
TAKES SHAPE
Goodbye, Billy

Monday, October 29, 1979. The Yankees unofficially began their 1980 season this week with the announcement that manager Billy Martin had been fired, once again. Yankee owner George Steinbrenner didn't waste much time on explanations or due process or even gauging fan reaction. Certainly the "investigations" that both Steinbrenner and Baseball Commissioner Bowie Kuhn announced cannot have run their courses, however cursory. Probably Steinbrenner was just looking for a way to get rid of Billy, and when one came along he jumped on it.

Not that it would have done Billy or the Yankees much good to have full-scale investigations carried on with the help of the press. Already we had been treated to the silliness of a 51-year-old man who deals with the press every day and is responsible for handling twenty-five athletes, saying that a man who followed him out of a hotel bar wound up with his face a bloody mess, requiring twenty stitches, because he slipped and fell and "cut his lip." "As I walked through the lobby I heard a noise. I turned around and saw a guy laying on the floor," said Martin.

With all the human tragedies around us, Martin's qualifies as one we do not have to take too seriously. In the tight world of baseball managers, Martin, despite five firings, has never been without a job for long, and his services will be sought again, sooner or later. It is also hard to see any human tragedy because Martin's life is lived on a cartoon level. After the incident, he showed up on Manhattan's East Side wearing cowboy boots and a cowboy hat and compared himself to the gunfighter who has an anonymous traveling salesman gunning for him in every bar in the West. The best part of this story, however, has got to be the identity of the man who finally brought Billy down. It was not one of your nasty young sportswriters who are always sniping at Billy. It was a 52-year-old marshmallow salesman. As in:

> *A marshmallow salesman named Cooper*
> *Thought Billy was drunk to a stupor,*
> *He neglected to duck*
> *When he said "Yankees suck,"*
> *And was felled by the skipper's last blooper.*

* * *

The Yankees' new manager will be Dick Howser, who is a noted teacher and should be a good manager for a young team. The Yankees, on the other hand, are an old team whose players have not shown any interest in being taught. Witness Howser's most famous moment as the Yankee third-base coach: the 1978 Reggie Jackson bunt. Howser relayed Martin's bunt sign when Reggie came to bat with a runner on first and the game tied in extra innings. Reggie, like so many power hitters today, can't bunt and considers it an insult to be asked. After one miss, Martin, via Howser, changed the sign, but the indignant Reggie continued to try to lay one down. Howser called him up the line and told him to swing away, and Reggie proceeded to bunt foul for strike three. It could be fun to bring up a college coach to manage the Yankees.

Wednesday, October 31, 1979. The Billy Affair is getting more and more sordid. Owner Steinbrenner was not content just to give Billy the axe, he twisted it in his back by letting on that he fired Billy to save his life, to keep Billy from future fights in which the drunk he attacked might have a gun or something. And Commissioner Kuhn, whose jurisdiction over the matter would evaporate, you would think, once Billy was no longer employed by a baseball team, announced on national TV that Billy had "financial problems," which prompted Billy's agent to threaten a libel suit against all concerned.

Now the marshmallow salesman gives his side of the story. He first wins my sympathy by acknowledging that everyone thinks it a big joke when they hear he is a marshmallow salesman. Then he shows that he is knowledgeable by saying the dispute started with his comment that Montreal Expo manager Dick Williams was a good choice as manager of the year over Earl Weaver. Billy's unreasonableness is shown by his belittling both rival managers. Then Billy pulls out five $100 bills (grotesque), bets them against Cooper's penny (obscene) that he can kick Cooper's butt (childish), and then decks Cooper with a sucker punch (miserable). Cooper refused to comment on Martin's state of inebriation and concluded, "It's a sad affair and I just want it to disappear." Fat chance of that.

Friday, November 9, 1979. Every year New York gets a new skyscraper, a defecting Russian ballet star, a previously unheard-of ethnic-day parade and, thanks to George Steinbrenner, a couple of free agents. This year Steinbrenner set a record with the speed in which he signed Bob Watson and Rudy May. And he's still fishing for the biggest catch of the year, Nolan Ryan. Steinbrenner landed the first big-money free agent, Catfish Hunter, five years ago and has continued to add big names to the Yankee roster every year since: Reggie Jackson, Don Gullett, Rich Gossage, Tommy John, Luis Tiant. He is quick to point out that he's not responsible for the system—and equally quick to imply that so long as the system sits there, you're stupid (or, probably worse, poor) if you don't take advantage of it. But the success of a team like Baltimore makes you think that there is more to winning baseball than assembling the best team money can buy.

The Watson signing, and the Yankee first-base situation in general, show how Steinbrenner and free agency are combining to destroy even the illusion of team loyalty that used to be part of the popular image of baseball. Bob Watson had played fourteen years for one club, the Houston Astros. When they decided that at age 33 he couldn't hit anymore, Boston took a chance on him and he proved he still could, at least in the American League, to the tune of .337. Now that he has proved his value, Steinbrenner has coaxed him away from the Red Sox, just as he did with Luis Tiant. Sure, the Red Sox had the chance to match the Yankees' offer, but what club in its right mind will pay a part-timer $375,000 a year—not just this year, but until he's 37 years old. But Steinbrenner "just looked over our budget for this year and realized that two and a half million people came out to see a fourth-place team . . . and gave us their hard-earned money." The ticket prices jumped up the year they signed Reggie and more people than ever showed up. Jack the prices up another dollar and bring in some more free agents. If Watson's hits net one win for the Yankees and they win their division by that one game, the signing will be a huge success financially, for Steinbrenner as well as for Watson.

But Watson has left the club where he enjoyed his best years, and he has left the club which gave him a second life. He has joined the ranks of baseball's ronin, the wandering samurai without a master, an identification, a loyalty. Bob Watson will never *be* a Yankee. He will be an Astro winding down his career in New York. He will never get the applause for a home run that Roy White has gotten for a mere appearance as a pinch runner.

Baseball fans are loyal, first to the team they support, second to the players who make up that team. Ideally, the two loyalties reinforce each other. A kid in Los Angeles would say that he likes Steve Garvey because he's a Dodger, and he likes the Dodgers because they have Steve Garvey. When a Tommy John leaves, it wrenches this civic identification, and the player and the team suffer in the public esteem. With some players, the identification is so strong that you hope they can stay with the team until it's time to quit—and you hope they know when that time comes.

A Yankee fan's loyalty is primarily to the organization. It has to be. The only current Yankee player, Roy White aside (where he will be soon), who has come up with the Yankees and has no other team identity is Ron Guidry. Steinbrenner must believe, no doubt correctly, that fans would rather win with purchased goods than come in second with homegrown stuff. He has assigned no value in his calculations to years of service in pinstripes. This was never clearer than last week when he unloaded Chris Chambliss for light-hitting catcher Rick Cerone from Toronto. Chambliss, of course, started with Cleveland, but in six years in New York he played day in, day out and became the closest thing to a fixture in the Yankee lineup of the '70s. His performance was more than routine: his home run against Kansas City to win the 1976 Playoffs was one of the most dramatic in Yankee history. But he became "expendable" the moment backup first baseman Jim Spencer signed a four-year contract at $300,000 a year.

If Spencer couldn't beat out Chambliss for the job on the field, how was he able to do it in the off-season? My hunch is that Spencer gave up his shot at the free-agent market for less money than Chambliss would have wanted next year, when he would be eligible to go that route. And Steinbrenner didn't want to lose Spencer this year and be forced to pay Chambliss twice as much next year or see him leave without a thank-you. Steinbrenner has lived by the free-agent sword long enough that he guards against its coming back to nick him. He knows he won't be able to appeal to any player's sense of team loyalty to stick with the Yankees. Loyalty didn't keep John with the Dodgers, Tiant with the Red Sox or Gullett with the Reds.

Saturday, November 10, 1979. Steinbrenner claims that in one week he has plugged four holes in the Yankee lineup, and two in the Yankee management. The question remaining is what are the plugs made of? From all reports, Ruppert Jones is no Mickey Rivers and Rick Cerone is no Thurman Munson. Bob Watson is being billed as a righthanded power hitter, but when was the last time such a species thrived in Yankee Stadium? And the only hole Rudy May is filling is the one, such as it is, left behind by Paul Mirabella. May announced he was ecstatic to be with the Yankees as a reliever, even though his beef with Montreal was that "my arm couldn't take it, pitching out of the bullpen—in my option year." Now that he's got his million, he should fit right in on the Yankees.

Tuesday, February 19, 1980. It is only mid-February, but the biggest news is the revival of the Billy and George show, with a new star in the supporting cast: Charlie Finley of the still-Oakland A's. What a great investment Billy Martin, Mgr., will be for Finley! In one move he will transform his collection of minor-leaguers from a team that passes through town unnoticed to a "scrappy bunch of unheralded hustlers led by peppery former Yankee, Billy Martin." Oakland games will be mentioned in the press for the first time in years. And can you imagine the tumult at Yankee Stadium when Billy the Kid brings out the lineup card! This move will be great for the rehabilitation of Martin, great for the credibility of the A's and great for the balance of the American League. And let no one overlook how great it will be for the Yankees: it gets Martin off their backs and sticks him on a club where he will increase attendance at Yankee games without a chance in the world of beating them.

The same day that the Martin rumors hit the papers came the official word that Roy White, the last of the last-place Yankees, has signed with the Yomiuri Giants of Tokyo. It is hard to believe that someone could play for the Yankees for fifteen years and remain as obscure and unsung as Roy White. His obscurity was largely deserved: he never batted .300, hit 25 homers or stole 25 bases, or led the league in anything besides at-bats and walks. His throwing arm, especially in later years, was pathetic. Even his position, leftfield, was obscure, cloaked with less Yankee tradition than the other eight. But Roy White was a survivor. Every year Yankee management took note of the above statistics and opened spring training with a new solution for the leftfield problem. But every September, there was Roy White, grounding a single up the middle or hooking a clutch home run just inside the foul pole. It took fifteen years for the fans to adopt Roy. In the final two months of 1979, every appearance by Roy as a pinch hitter or pinch runner was greeted with a standing ovation. Some of the gesture was simply a matter of taking his side against the insensitive Yankee management—a management that produced a fourth-place team in '79. Mostly, though, it was a way of giving a "Day" to someone who had played more games as a Yankee than anyone except Mantle, Gehrig, Ruth and Berra. Roy White was not in their class as a player. But he was a decent man who stood out among his teammates for his self-effacement. He will be, I suspect, a perfect Japanese.

Thursday, March 20. Spring has officially arrived, and there are two questions to be resolved in the three weeks between now and Opening Day: which nine pitchers will make the Yankee squad and will there, because of the stalemated contract talks, even be an Opening Day?

The four marginal pitchers battling for the one open spot on the staff are rookies Dave Righetti and Mike Griffin, perennial prospect Ken Clay and wily veteran Jim Kaat.

Righetti and Griffin are rated so highly that the Yankees re-
fused to trade either one last week for Don Sutton, the Dodgers' all-time winningest pitcher and a sure 18-game winner
for the Yanks in '80. Of course, such a deal would have given
New York the oldest pitching staff in major league history, not
to mention the half dozen most independent-minded hurlers
this side of Steve Carlton. Clay, meanwhile, is walking reproof
of what happens to live-armed prospects who are kept around
and run up against the Yankees' high-priced veteran starters.
As for Kaat, if he makes the team he will have played in the
majors during four different decades. For this reason, mainly,
I'm rooting for Kaat—it's a shot at making history that, like
some kind of eclipse, occurs only every ten years. There will
be plenty of time for Righetti and Griffin and once again no
time, I suspect, for Clay. This time, let's go with Kaat.

It is also true that Kaat hardly seems like a Yankee. He
pitched for so long with the Phillies and then the Twins that
his Yankee uniform looks merely borrowed. His stubby glove
and no-windup delivery increase the impression that he is out
of place. And finally, the willingness and dispatch with which
he will trot in to face one batter and then leave without
throwing his glove in disgust makes him the ultimate odd-
man-out on any team of the '80s, let alone the Yankees.

In fact, everything Jim Kaat does on the field makes you
think not so much of a Yankee worth serious detesting but of
a journeyman pitcher of the '50s yanked from his present
obscurity selling insurance for a turn on the mound during
the Old-Timers' Game. Where have you gone, Bobby Shantz?

Thursday, April 3. The Grapefruit and Cactus Leagues folded
early this year. The players, intent on showing the owners
the lengths to which they will go to retain the present free-
agent system, have announced they will play no more spring
training exhibition games. At least I will avoid the false hopes
that the spring training standings have provided me since the

mid-'50s, when the ultimately abysmal Pittsburgh Pirates invariably led the league and the inevitably champion Yankees wound up somewhere near the bottom. Despite the manager's annual protestation that spring training games didn't mean a damn, I continued to see impending doom when, on the trip north, a college team here or a minor league team there would trip up the New Yorkers. What did Casey know that I didn't?

Sunday, April 6. Unlike the Mets, who bolted as soon as the strike was called, seemingly to escape the embarrassment of the upcoming season, most of the Yankees have stayed in spring training camp, where they are working out under the manager's supervision. There are exceptions, most importantly Ron Guidry. His absence is being explained by his wife's pregnancy, but those of us looking for cracks attribute his departure to his personal contract grievances with Yankee management. What he's saying, in his quietly fast way, is no more Mr. Nice Guy, no more team man who will volunteer for bullpen duty and start the big game on two days' rest. Ron Guidry is looking out for himself a little more from here on in.

The only other big development is Reggie's idea that the players indicate they are on strike by refusing to wear the tops of their uniforms. Since this keeps down the laundry bill, management is not going to fight this one.

Tuesday, April 8. I left my baseball card collection to Harvard College twelve years ago. Or left it *at,* if we are being technical. My roommate and I wallpapered our college suite with our childhood collections, *circa* 1954–59, stapling the cards together in vertical strips and suspending the strips from glued-on picture hangers. We even assembled the 1955 Bowman series, in which each player's face was framed in a TV set, into a large rectangle itself representing a TV set, with the middle of the screen reserved for the collection's crown jewels, the Mistake Cards. Bowman had put out cards for Frank Bolling and Milt Bolling, brother infielders for the Tigers and Red Sox, except that on some of these cards, the fronts and backs were mixed up, and Frank Bolling's picture had Milt Bolling's statistics on the back. We had all heard stories of the famous postage stamp with the upside-down airplane and how many thousands it was worth. Well here, it seemed, was the 1955 equivalent, bound to be extremely valuable someday.

When we graduated, the cards stayed behind, partly from our desire to establish an Eliot House C-41 legacy and partly because no one wanted to remove four thousand staples. Several summers later, I regret to say, the cards disappeared, presumably at the hands of the university painters.

I didn't think much about baseball cards after that. Oh, each new year I would rhapsodize a little about how the smell of bubble gum in the air was as much a harbinger of spring as the first crocus or robin. Occasionally I would see a new model card on the sidewalk and would reflect how cluttered, how tacky it looked compared to the classic elegance of the 1954 Topps series. But all thoughts of collecting, the chief vice of my youth, were gone.

Then in Friday's *New York Post* two weeks ago I saw an announcement that the New York Superstar Baseball Card convention would be held that weekend at the Prince George Hotel on 28th Street, with auctions, memorabilia, card-flipping contests and autograph-signing appearances by ex-Dodger Carl Erskine on Saturday and ex-Yankee Elston Howard on Sunday. I had never been to a baseball card convention or talked to a major-leaguer, or for that matter ever been to 28th Street, so I headed downtown on Sunday a bit like I was approaching a black hole, or at least a Star Trek reunion. Actually, I doubted that I would find more than twenty people, and none of them over the age of thirteen, so I fully expected to have to carry the conversational load with Ellie. I therefore began to plan my questions in advance.

Howard had been the first black on the Yankees, and offhand I couldn't remember his appearing on many baseball cards. (In the old days not every player had a baseball card: in 1954 Ted Williams started and ended the Topps series with cards number 1 and 250.) "Were you," I could break the ice by asking, "discriminated against, Ellie, by the baseball card companies?"

Or I could ask him about something Phil Rizzuto let slip on the first telecast of spring training. Commenting on Howard's move this year from the coaching ranks to the Yankee front office, Rizzuto said, "Ellie didn't want to take off the pinstripes, but George thought he'd be more valuable as his right-hand man." Maybe I could get a clarification: "Phil said you got a promotion but aren't happy about it, Ellie. Why's that? Is George as big a bastard to work for as everyone says? Or is it that you'd just rather do nothing on the field than in an office?"

But if by chance there were more than twenty people and there was only time for one question, it would have to be about a game Ellie played in Yankee Stadium in August 1967 *against* the Yankees. After thirteen years in pinstripes, the 38-year-old Howard was shipped off to finish his career with the Red Sox. In his first game against his old team he guided two 23-year-old pitchers, Dave Morehead and an obscure rookie named Sparky Lyle, to a five-hit shutout, he drove in one of the three Boston runs, and he threw out Mickey Mantle trying, despite his crippled legs, to steal second. "What did it feel like, Ellie," I would goad him, "to humiliate the New York Yankees?"

On the off-chance I wouldn't get to talk to Howard, I figured I could at least find out what my Bollings would have been worth.

I arrived at the hotel at 12:30. The man paying $3 in front of me asked the ticket seller, "Is Elston Howard here? I only came to see Elston Howard." The lady said he would be coming but she didn't know when. My carefully planned conversation with the ex-Yankee backstop lurched out the window when I got my hand stamped and passed into the hotel's Grand Ballroom. More than eighty booths were crammed into the place and hundreds of people—young boys, young men, young fathers, young wives—were shouldering their way through the maze, turning over Lucite pages loaded with cards, asking for '58 Henry Aarons.

Some booths were manned by Pop and Mom, with Junior in a baseball cap sitting alongside. These booths often featured other memorabilia: a 10-cent program from the 1948 Giants-Cardinals football game was being offered for $6. Other booths were the domain of pure professionals: cards only and instant answers to all questions.

Robert Thing belonged to the latter group. From Skowhegan, Maine, he rode the Northeast circuit that took him to a different convention every weekend. He boasted a stock of a million cards—not counting his side business in 1980 cards. These he bought directly from the Topps factory; you could buy from him an unsorted box of 500 for $6, or for $13 you could buy a complete set, presorted by his assistants back home, numbers 1 to 762. A boy came by with a stack of about 200 old cards from the '50s. "I can give you $5," offered Thing. "They're almost all commons and I've got six or seven of most of them already."

The money is in the "stars," the names everybody knows, and nothing helps prices like admission to the Hall of Fame. A 1952 Mickey Mantle is the 1909 SVDB of the game, fetching, this year, around $3,000. Those Ted Williams cards from 1954 go for $50 apiece. Spahn, Mays, Kaline, Clemente are other big items—especially in their rookie years, when fewer cards were made and fewer saved. It surprised me, but I guess it is somehow just that players obscure in their primes should remain obscure in the hobbyists' history books. Bud Podbielan will not achieve a latter-day fame because his baseball card is scarce. And Bollings, even without staple holes, were being sold for only $2.50.

On special occasions, of course, a common may go like a star: practically all Elston Howard cards had been snapped up in anticipation of his autograph session. Other collectors had brought baseballs for the same purpose. I was already enough of a tourist clogging up the selling lanes; imagine how out of place I would be in the autograph line. "While you're autographing this return-fare subway ticket for me, Mr. Howard, could you answer one question . . ." Then around 1:30 the half-expected announcement came over the ballroom loudspeaker. "Unfortunately, we have just learned that due to illness Elston Howard is not able to come today. In his place, Carl Erskine will start signing autographs in the Baroque Room at two o'clock."

I had already overheard cracks about the $500 fee Howard was to receive for a one-hour appearance. The reactions to this announcement were in the same vein: "His illness is probably so bad he can't get off the golf course." Another man, more resigned than indignant, said to a vendor: "I drove 100 miles with my two kids to see Elston Howard. They've never heard of Carl Erskine. This makes such a bad impression. Even if Howard *is* sick, half the people here wouldn't believe it." It was bad enough that someone was getting $500 just to sign his name for an hour. It was worse that he didn't even show up—and that somebody withheld the no-show announcement until all the day's admissions had been paid. For this was not just a visit to nostalgia; this was also a business. "Mickey Mantle gets $3,500 to appear at these things," someone said, "and he's booked solid. We tried to get him and couldn't."

Mantle does have his standards, however. He declined Billy Martin's offer to make him a coach for the Oakland A's. The Mick couldn't see wearing one of those green and gold uniforms (which probably would have been the extent of his duties), although two more years would have given him twenty on his baseball pension, which "would be a help," he said. What "help" Mantle needs when there are baseball card conventions around the country all year long beats me. As for Elston Howard, the experience made me wonder what exactly his new job is with the Yankees. I won't be surprised if when I open my first 1980 scorecard he is listed in the executive hierarchy, several lines below George Steinbrenner, with some grand title . . . like Vice President, Public Relations.

Chapter 2
PLAY BALL!
Who Counts the
First Month Anyway?

Thursday, April 10. How great to have the season open and what a great season opener! I have seldom seen a baseball game move so fast, as Ron Guidry and the Rangers' Jon Matlack cruised through nine scoreless innings in less than an hour and fifty minutes. In fact, I made only one baseball note to myself, under the heading Trends to Watch For in 1980, when third baseman Graig Nettles booted two ground balls. In a preseason show I heard Nettles blame last year's fielding slump on his glove's being stolen at the All-Star Game. He ominously added that the replacement glove it had taken him the second half of last season to break in was also stolen, early in spring training.

I didn't have to wait long for that trend to develop. In fact, an hour later it turned out to be the only difference between Texas and the Yankees. For both teams the lefty aces pitched nine scoreless innings without a walk, the right-handed flame-throwing relievers (Kern and Gossage) were wild, the backup lefty relievers (Lyle and Underwood) were effective, and one batter (Sundberg and Watson) got three of the team's four hits. But in the twelfth inning Nettles couldn't react in time to a one-hopper by Mickey Rivers that bounced off his chest, and in panic he threw the ball away. After a sacrifice and two intentional walks, rookie manager Dick Howser brought in Rich Gossage to face Richie Zisk. The broadcasters didn't want to second-guess Howser in his first game, but they did mention that Gossage is usually wild early in the season. They mentioned that Zisk beat Gossage and the Yanks with a home run in a similar situation two years ago. And they pointed out, throughout the game, that the morning paper in Dallas had quoted Zisk as saying, "If we can stay close against Guidry for six innings, we'll beat Gossage." They didn't have time to mention that new Yankee catcher Rick Cerone had caught Gossage only one inning in spring training, and that Gossage's fastball gets to the plate a lot quicker than the pitches Underwood had been throwing. Cerone just wasn't ready for Gossage's first fastball, low and outside. It bounced off his glove and Rivers scooted home with the night's only run.

Friday, April 11. The same teams can play the same sport of baseball on consecutive days in the same park and produce two entirely different games. Tonight's 11–7 Ranger win had little of anything, except drama, in common with Opening Night's neatly played 1–0 jewel of a game. If the Yankees can manage to lose both low-scoring games and slugfests, there is hope for this season.

Saturday, April 12. Today's rainout in Texas will result in the season's first, and perhaps only, Sunday afternoon doubleheader tomorrow. Sunday afternoon doubleheaders are, or at least were, a traditional part of the month of July, when you can listen to the second game on your way home from the beach. An April doubleheader is nothing but a freak.

WPIX, the Yankee television station, filled the sudden hole in its schedule with the same swashbuckler movie it puts on every time there is a rainout, so I switched over to NBC's Game of the Week. It pitted the Houston Astros against the overexposed Los Angeles Dodgers. The Dodger infield is starting its eighth year intact, and it sure is hard to get excited by them anymore. I left the game for good, I thought, with the score tied 5–5 in the ninth. Who really cared? A couple of hours later I turned the TV on again—and there were the Dodgers and Astros, still playing! More interesting than the outcome of the game, at least to announcer Joe Garagiola, was what NBC was going to do with the regularly scheduled Saturday night show "B.J. and the Bear." It got canceled, the Astros lost in the seventeenth inning, and NBC remained a distant third in the ratings race.

Sunday, April 13. Baseball-to-do-the-taxes-by is about what the Yankees and Rangers played, for six and a half hours today. The Yankees won two games by big margins, 9–4 and 8–2, as much because of Texas sloppiness as Yankee power. Nothing to get excited about, or worried about: the Yankees, so far, are playing just .500 ball.

The best play of the day involved the three Yankee outfielders. With one out and the speedy Ruppert Jones on third and the equally swift Bobby Brown on first, Reggie Jackson lofted a long fly to Rusty Staub in left. Both runners tagged, Staub's throw came in to second and Brown, for reasons not apparent on the instant replay, was called out. For reasons that *were* clear, however, the home plate umpire ruled that Jones's run did not count. He had stopped running the last two steps and was watching the play at second as he walked absentmindedly across the plate. Thus Jackson did not get his first RBI of the year and, just as bad, he was charged with a time at bat. It's a play to remember in case Reggie ends up hitting .299 with 99 RBIs.

Tuesday, April 15. The Reggie Jackson Sideshow for 1980 has already begun. There were only 6,000 fans in Comiskey Park tonight to watch the first game of the year between the Yankees and the White Sox, but they managed to put together several very audible chants of "Reg-gie sucks" when number 44 came to the plate.

Now I am not a fan of "suck" cheers. I was first exposed to this form of expression at a Columbia-Harvard basketball game four years ago, where "Harvard sucks" seemed to be the most effective verbal assault Ivy League education was producing. Not only did the sentiment ring false, the wit seemed deficient in contrast to the slightly more clever cheers of my college days, such as the football chant, "Repel them/ Repel them/Makethemrelinquishtheball." Shortly thereafter, the "suck" cheer, which has the virtue of being easily adaptable to any sport and any occasion, showed up in Yankee Stadium in honor of the visiting Boston Red Sox. On the evidence of its public appearances, the word "suck" is now probably one of the ten commonest words in elementary schools around the country and is probably no more offensive to the younger generation than "You stink" was in my time. (Then again, my mother wasn't too keen on "stinks" in those days, either.) But despite the increasing exposure to it at sporting events, society's mainstream still refuses to acknowledge the "suck" cheer, a policy followed by the Yankee announcers when the sound pounded through their microphones to those listening at home.

I can see two excuses for this lapse of good manners by the White Sox fans. One is that it was forty degrees and sleeting today and snowed the day before in Chicago, forcing a postponement of the series opener. Anyone who had braved the weather, and then sat through extra innings, was entitled to carry on a little, if only to warm up the empty ballpark. The second excuse is Reggie Jackson. Reggie got off to a slow start in Texas, but to the discerning eye it was clear he had not lost his knack of doing things just a little differently and attracting the world's notice. When he finally hit his first homer, he managed to miss first base on his home-run trot; so, halfway to second he came back to first, retouched it, and continued his trot, managing to lengthen an already long moment and give the cameras and announcers more time to linger on his achievement.

Against the Sox, Reggie got a single and once at first base proceeded to engage in a five-second soul shake with Chicago first baseman Lamar Johnson. Now, maybe Reggie hadn't seen Lamar all winter and was just saying Happy New Year, or maybe he was congratulating Lamar for being named American League Player of the Week today. Who am I to criticize a friendly gesture? It's just that in all my years of baseball watching, I have *never* seen the batter shake the first baseman's hand after reaching first base with a single. Such a gesture, of course, was against baseball's nonfraternization rules for many years. Now that the rules have been eased, is Reggie Jackson spearheading a new spirit of team detente? I doubt it, since when he came around to score he didn't shake the catcher's hand or even run across the plate as normal people do. No, he jumped in the air and landed on the plate with both feet, even though a bat was lying across it.

In short, Reggie was just being Reggie, being Mr. Nice Guy in a way that constantly puts him in the spotlight and causes people to misunderstand him or, in the case of the chanting Chicago fans, think him an asshole.

Thursday, April 17. The White Sox took the rubber game of their series with the Yankees and in the process may have doomed Jim Kaat. The Sox were already winning 5–4 when Kaat gave up his three runs, but when you don't have a future to offer you can't afford too many slipups in the present. It never seemed likely, anyway, that a team with pennant pretensions would have Jim Kaat, Rudy May *and* Tom Underwood in its bullpen.

Today's game started at the strange hour of 4:45 because league rules don't allow a night game on a travel day when a team has a game scheduled the next afternoon. Chicago owner Bill Veeck didn't reschedule the game, which had been snowed out Monday night, for a more normal 1:30 or 2 o'clock start because, he said, he didn't want to compete with the Cubs' home opener and hoped to pick up some fans on their way home from Wrigley Field, which is only on the opposite side of Chicago. George Steinbrenner, like Reggie Jackson, sees the world in mostly personal terms, and claimed that the late start was chosen by Veeck purely to interfere with the Welcome Home Dinner planned for the Yankees in New York that evening. Why Veeck would give a damn about something that no one else cared about—except the players who traditionally get fined for skipping the event—was not clear. What was fairly clear was that Veeck ended up with what sounded on the radio like the same 6,000 fans who had been yelling obscenities at Reggie all week.

At game's end they joined in what I consider to be the league's most original and best cheer, one that even Reggie—after three games in the muck and cold before a small but hostile crowd—could have gladly joined in: "Nana-na-na, nana-na-na, hey-hey-hey, good-bye."

Saturday, April 19. Washington, D.C., doesn't have an American League team anymore—or yet, as the case may be—but it does have federal regulation with tentacles that reach into every field of endeavor, including our national pastime. So even though I am spending a spring weekend away from New York, and am missing the Brewers' first visit of the year, I was able to get my daily dosage of baseball by tracking down an exhibit at the National Archives called Baseball as Business.

The exhibit was drawn from the Federal Trade Commission's 1962 case against the Topps Chewing Gum Company, alleging a monopoly in the baseball card–bubble gum industry. The elements of the lawsuit were compared to a baseball game and were illustrated with pictures of Yankees: the complaint equaled the pitch (Whitey Ford), the hearing examiner equaled the umpire (arguing with Yogi Berra). On the bottom ledge were assorted baseball cards, and pinned to the display boards were various documents filed in the case: the Topps exclusive contract, letters to the players, a Topps interoffice memo reporting on who signed up at the Yankee camp that day ("Bobby Richardson was about to sign, but Frank Crosetti called him to the bus." "Bill Skowron signed and selected a home movie camera.") The suspense built until the final showcase: would the FTC find a monopoly?

It seemed clear to me, even before I went to law school, that there is a monopoly in baseball cards. Oh sure, for a couple of years back in the '50s there was a competing Bowman series. But that quickly and mysteriously disappeared and the words "Topps" and "baseball cards" have since been synonymous.

The hearing examiner agreed and found Topps to be in violation of the antitrust laws. But when his opinion was appealed to the full FTC, it was reversed by the baseball score of 4–1. In a neat bit of definitional dancing, the Commission said that Topps did not have a monopoly because the Topps contract covered only "confectionery product" sales. The players were still free to sell their pictures to cereal, bottle cap, and T-shirt companies, examples of whose wares were also on display. Similarly, Topps didn't have a monopoly of the bubble gum business. Lots of gum was being sold with Beatles cards, and even without cards of any kind! So Topps could continue paying players a paltry $125 a year for the right to turn their pictures into money.

Monday, April 21. When the American League pennant winners for the last two years meet for the first time in the season and start their second-best pitchers, you can expect a good baseball game, and that's what we got tonight when the Orioles came to town. My current definition of a good baseball game is one that is not only close and exciting but gives you some why-didn't-he's to think about afterward. Baseball is a game of inches, but so are golf and horseracing. The physical performances are important, but it is the mental dimension that allows us our second guesses and makes the sport so endlessly fascinating.

My second-guessing Monday night devolved on a defensive nonplay by Oriole first baseman Eddie Murray. With the score tied 2–2 in the bottom of the eighth and Mike Flanagan and Tommy John locked in the anticipated pitchers' duel, Rick Cerone led off with a single. Everyone in the park was expecting a sacrifice bunt from Bucky Dent, including the Baltimore defense. The bunt went down the first-base line and the charging Murray scooped it up cleanly and turned to look at second base. Cerone was only halfway from first when Murray turned, but he didn't throw! He turned back toward first, waited a couple of beats and lobbed a throw to retire Dent by five steps. One out later Ruppert Jones hit a grounder past Murray, appropriately enough, to drive in Cerone with the winning run. The ball eluded Murray by a matter of inches, but it wasn't that closeness that made the game, for this spectator, a good one. It was the play that set it up, and my belief that were it not for Murray's throw to the wrong base, the game would still be tied.

Tuesday, April 22. Tonight's Oriole-Yankee game was just as close as last night's but not as good. I must amend the definition that came to mind after the Yankees' 3–2 win Monday to add that a "good" game must also be reasonably well played. For starters, Monday's game was played in one hour fifty-two minutes. Tonight's took three hours sixteen minutes. Rookie pitcher Mike Griffin went to three-ball counts on four batters in the first inning alone, and there were four Oriole wild pitches in the game. The big question that the game threatened to pose for analysis was: should the runner on third in a bases-loaded situation slide or run across the plate when the batter hits a ground ball? Benny Ayala, who is a generally terrible baseball player, slid home and was called out by a matter of inches. Since the Orioles were behind 2–1 in the sixth inning, this loomed as a potentially decisive play. Any discussion of this point, however, was immediately made moot when Willie Randolph dropped a popup and three runs scored. That play, in turn, raised other questions, but ones without the same general application. Such as: how in the world could an official scorer call a dropped popup a double?

Friday, April 25. Give the Yankees a day off and the New York sportswriters will use it to come up with a discontented player. It's the Yankee style of sportswriting, ingrained forever, it seems, during the year of Reggie's arrival and the "Bronx Zoo" season that followed. At one time or another during those two years, every player on the Yankees said he wanted to be somewhere else; for the writers it was just a matter of spacing out the complaints so that there would be a fresh story each week.

They have been looking for this kind of story, which they can write in their sleep, since the season turned into its second week. The first candidate was Nettles, who had a horrendous start both in the field and at bat and was so upset when he was removed for a pinch hitter that he shattered the lights in the clubhouse runway. This week's candidate is Bobby Murcer. Murcer's job is to sit on the bench and personify the Yankees' awesome depth. But as soon as he came up with a game-winning hit against Baltimore on Tuesday—two innings after grounding into a bases-loaded doubleplay his first time up—the reporters were ready to pounce. "Nice hit, Bobby. . . . How's it feel to come off the bench and win the game? . . . Do you think you'll get a chance to play more now? . . . Are you happy with your backup role this year?" is how I imagine the sequence of questioning went. Everybody knows how Murcer—or almost any other major-leaguer—would answer those questions ("Thanks. . . . Great. . . . I hope so. . . . Not really"). The reporters are not looking for answers, they're looking for an issue.

The opening gambit was contained in Wednesday's *New York Post:* "So, it now must be asked [must?], will Murcer see more action?" By the Friday *New York Times,* when there was no game to report, the "issue" had grown to a full story with the headline "Murcer Is Unhappy Over Seat on Bench."

No one suggests there is any place for him but the bench. Put him in center and you're messing with the Yankees' commitment to the future, Ruppert Jones. Take Reggie out of right and you're asking for a full-scale revolution. You've already got three people—Oscar Gamble, Lou Piniella and Bobby Brown—fighting over left, two of whom will be unhappy. Which leaves Murcer battling Jim Spencer for the lefthanded DH spot—not a big opening on a team that faces mostly lefthanded pitchers.

So no one is really second-guessing Howser, no one is explaining why the Yankees have lost six of their first thirteen games, and no one is really feeling sorry for Murcer, whom the lowly Cubs didn't want and who is being paid a phenomenal $320,000 this year and next. Nor is anyone really reporting a piece of news. The pack of journalists who cover the Yankees are just filing on what they see as a routine story angle from the Yankee clubhouse: who might be unhappy today?

Monday, April 28. The sportswriters have now caught some bigger fish in their nets of discontent. Their first cast in the waters brought up Nettles and Murcer. The latter stopped splashing when George Steinbrenner implied none too subtly that if Murcer didn't shut up, the Yankees would dump him —treatment easier to apply to the aging, overpaid outfield reserve than to their starting third baseman. Next, the *Post's* Mike Marley went after Bobby Brown, basing a saga of disquiet mostly on his interpretation of Brown's word "funky."

Not content to be typecast as a defensive caddy or pinch runner, wanting a chance to show what he could do, too old to have to sit around and wait for a break anymore, etc. Small stuff. Sardines.

Now on Monday, absolutely burying all news of another 2-hour, 14-minute masterpiece by Tommy John, 1–0 over the White Sox, comes an ultimatum from pitcher Ed Figueroa: trade me in ten days, "even to the Mets," or I'm going back to Puerto Rico. Admittedly, we have heard this before from Figgy. Except when he has been pitching every four days and shooting to become the first 20-game winner from Puerto Rico, he has been unhappy with the Yankees. He, and therefore his complaints, were just never quite as important as those of Rivers, Reggie Jackson, Nettles, Munson and Lyle. This time, however, the press is behaving like we have a major media event on our hands. As for me, I'll believe it when I see it. No matter how injured and ineffective Figueroa has been recently, the Yankees aren't going to commit the fourth spot in the rotation to Underwood or Griffin just yet. And no matter how unhappy players are, they have a way of not getting out of George's camp until he is ready to unload them. But the pack of reporters covering the Yankees has, only sixteen games into the season, succeeded in roiling the waters, and you can be sure they will have their hooks out the rest of the way.

Tuesday, April 29. The Yankees traveled to Baltimore yesterday. By Thursday they will have played two series with Baltimore before they have faced nine other teams even once. And their other games with Baltimore are scheduled for the middle of August, which is about when the Orioles each year miraculously turn into a great team. So for the last seven weeks of the 1980 season it is possible that there could be two pennant races going in the East—one in Baltimore, one in New York—and the two principals would never meet. What a shame.

The good thing about road games, to my mind, is that they usually start at 7:30. The Yankees' 8:00 P.M. starting time leaves two or three hours to get ready for the game, but who needs that? And in contrast to the theater or movies, where you need to eat dinner *before* an 8 o'clock show time, hot dogs and beer invariably taste better when the moon is up and the game is under way. Even worse than the wasted time at the start of the evening is the fact that an eight o'clock game at Yankee Stadium doesn't get over until 10:30 or 11:00, which means I am riding the subway home with a thousand other exhausted fans when I really would like to be getting ready for bed.

Last night the 7:30 start in Baltimore enabled the teams to get in four innings before the rain started in earnest. And if the Orioles had been leading, there might even have been time for more. As it was, the last ten minutes of what turned out to be a nongame and the first five minutes of the rain delay proved to be the highlights of my day.

The weather was terrible all along the East Coast and rain was forecast in Baltimore all evening, but the Orioles had a big advance sale, and the Yankees are in town only twice all year, so they started the game. When Jim Palmer gave up a triple and double to Ruppert Jones, a single to Gamble and a homer to Reggie in the first three innings for a 4–0 lead, Baltimore—that is, Earl Weaver's—strategy quickly shifted. Weaver started to slow things down with an unnecessary visit to the mound by his pitching coach, then—unheard of— he kept his players in the dugout before the start of the fifth inning. The umpires finally ordered them out, and they complied, slowly. Then the umps changed their mind and called out the ground crew, which applauded the decision like good hometown fans and proceeded to cover the field with the concern and speed of a turtle.

The best thing was the way Weaver had gotten the Yankees' goat again. Not only was Howser out on the field complaining—along with, as you might expect, Reggie Jackson—

but Elston Howard dropped by the broadcast booth to make the point to Frank Messer and the TV audience that baseball should really do something about these tactics of Earl Weaver. So maybe this is Ellie's new job that I was wondering about: hit man for George Steinbrenner?

Not only did the rain erase a win for the Yankees, it wiped out a Jackson home run and a possible victory for rookie Mike Griffin, whom I had just denigrated to Jimmy, our apartment doorman, as no more promising than Ken Clay or Jim Beattie. It also avoided what might have been a comical fifth inning, with Howser trying to get his hitters to make quick outs and Weaver urging his pitchers to have trouble finding the plate. Would such team players as Gamble and Jackson, the first two Yankees due up, have sacrificed an at-bat to the cause? We'll never know.

Thursday, May 1. Figgy has abandoned his threat of going to Puerto Rico and forfeiting his pay—no surprise there—but he has not given up his request for a trade. The justification for his walkout—that the Yankees are not pitching him enough—is so standard that we hardly give it a second thought. But it is a prime example of the sports world's modern personnel headache, "selfism," putting your own interests before those of your team.

The condition can take many forms, to judge from a glance at today's sports page. Pittsburgh pitcher Bert Blyleven has demanded to be traded because having a manager take him out of games "too early" has, to quote the team's vice president, "affected his everyday life and his effectiveness as a pitcher." And Atlanta slugger Bob Horner, who had just signed a three-year contract for a million dollars, decided he would rather quit baseball than let owner Ted Turner snap him out of a slump by sending him to the minors. Also yesterday, the Milwaukee Bucks announced the retirement of basketball star Dave Meyers to devote his services to Jehovah's Witnesses. And then there is football star Jack Tatum. He at least still wants to play, but doesn't seem to recognize the inconsistency between participating in a team sport and publishing a book about himself titled, *They Call Me Assassin.* The Oakland Raiders traded Tatum yesterday to the Houston Oilers for two waterboys and some extra kicking tees.

The day before the Raiders had acquired safety Burgess Owens, who was allegedly considered expendable by the New York Jets because he was preparing a study on racism in the NFL.

A somewhat more romantic and selfless view of sports was inculcated in me early by my father. But my confirmation in this religion came in tenth grade, when I was a substitute forward on my prep school's JV basketball team. Our coach was named Merrill Shanks and the word was he had been a Little All-America at a small Ohio college the year before. I was solidly anchored on the third team when I got an invitation to winter-weekend at a girls' school even more remote from civilization than my own. Going away for a weekend sounded pretty cool and would restore some ego bruised from spending the last two weekends on the bench. Since Mr. Shanks didn't think enough of my basketball skills to use me in the games, I didn't see how he could object to my skipping one. So I asked him, and he answered with what may be the only words I remember from that year, or even that prep school: "Either you're a member of the team or you're not, and if you're a member of the team I expect you at every game."

I was crushed. Not because I would miss the dance. But because Mr. Shanks's answer seemed so right, and I had not thought of it myself.

Saturday, May 3. The ultimatum of Ed Figueroa, not surprisingly, has ended with a fizzle, not a trade. He will stay in New York and collect his free-agent pot of gold at the end of the season, and if Howser wants to use him in relief, that's okay. "Whatever I said, I'm sorry," the *Times* quotes the

31-year-old righthander as saying. If "whatever I said" is supposed to include his comments Thursday about being traded to the National League, Figueroa will not get off easy, at least not in my book. According to the *Post,* Figgy said: "I don't want to go to the National League. I don't want to go through running bases and bunting."

Can you believe it? The guy is paid $130,000 a year for playing baseball—and he doesn't even like playing baseball. Running bases. Bunting. Presumably swinging a bat on occasion also, although Figgy forgot that part. Can you imagine if that were the bad part of your job?

Monday, May 5. Reggie and the Beanball, Part 1. On July 27, 1979, the day I started this diary, Cecil Cooper hit the first of his three home runs in the first inning. When he came to bat in the third inning, he was decked by Ed Figueroa. The first Yankee batter to face Brewer pitcher Mike Caldwell in the top of the fourth was Reggie Jackson. Caldwell's first pitch, high and tight, returned Figueroa's message. No surprise. Then with the count two balls and two strikes, Caldwell decked Jackson again. Reggie was not so angry that he put his bat down and immediately attacked Caldwell. No, Reggie stayed up there to take his cut on the 3–2 pitch, realizing, no doubt, that a 400-foot clout would be his best revenge. When he popped up to the third baseman, however, that avenue of revenge was closed off, so Reggie tossed his bat toward the mound. That's not part of generally accepted baseball practices, but it was apparently all that Reggie could think of on the spot. After having more time to consider the matter as he ran out the popup, he embarked on a more normal course: he charged the mound and proceeded to throttle the pitcher. Reggie caused no grave physical harm, but he did precipitate a bench-clearing melee that resulted in a full-page picture spread in the next day's *Post* featuring closeups of, you guessed it, Reggie Jackson.

Reggie and the Beanball, Part 2. I was reminded of Reggie's Retaliation last Friday when I assured a *Time* Magazine researcher that reference to the incident in a forthcoming essay on "Revenge" would not be libelous. *Time*'s essay, pegged to events in Iran, made the point that whatever use this basic human emotion may have as a guiding principle in baseball, it should not be a cornerstone of American foreign policy.

Then two days later I found myself brushed back by a déjà vu fastball from Minnesota Twins pitcher Jerry Koosman. In the second inning of Sunday's game, Koosman threw a high hard one and Reggie crashed backward to the ground. I don't think Kooz was necessarily throwing at Reggie, but of course Reggie did, and he bitched at catcher Butch Wynegar. Broadcaster Bill White thought it a beanball, too, and he proclaimed that the Yankee pitcher, Tommy Underwood, would have to retaliate when the Twins came to bat. The next pitch was also inside, but it was a slow curve, the kind a .200 hitter would love to get hit by. But Reggie's no .200 hitter and he took a few steps out toward the mound. Third-base coach Mike Ferraro raced in to restrain Reggie and then had to push Reggie away from the home plate umpire, who apparently didn't share Jackson's view that Koosman should be disciplined.

If a brushback pitch is supposed to intimidate the batter, it was having the opposite effect here. Jackson seemed to be intimidating the umpire, and he certainly was affecting Koosman, who had to stand lamely on the mound, his rhythm destroyed, his control of the game taken away from him while Jackson carried on like a bull elephant being attacked by Marlin Perkins. The game began again only when Reggie was ready, and my worst fears were confirmed two pitches later when Jackson hit a slider on the low outside corner 443 feet into the centerfield bleachers.

For all intents and purposes the game was over. Reggie's sheer act of will, however distasteful, had destroyed Koosman's confidence and the Twins remained in a shell all the way to a 10–1 loss. Underwood, who is trying desperately to earn a spot in the starting rotation, neglected to throw at any-body next inning, despite constant egging on by Bill White and Frank Messer. Somebody must have gotten to him in the dug-out before the next inning, however, for he planted a fastball in Wynegar's back to lead off the third. The demands of base-ball's code of honor had been satisfied.

The Twins fell apart in the fourth, but let's watch Reggie, as the TV camera did, as he goes around the bases for one of New York's six runs that inning: Reggie lines a single to left and points at the Twins dugout, seemingly yelling, "Take that, you epithets," to someone who has been riding him at the plate. The shortstop makes a good stop on a grounder but his toss goes behind the second baseman covering the bag. Reg-gie only has eyes for the second baseman, however, and levels him with a slide that doesn't hit the ground until Reggie is past second base. "Nothing dirty about that," Rizzuto says approvingly as Reggie scrambles back to second before some-one can pick up the ball and tag him out. On third base Reg-gie removes his glasses and tosses them to Ferraro—while Koosman is in the middle of his delivery! Piniella's single to right scores Reggie, but his inning's not over. When Koosman throws one inside to Nettles, Reggie is off the bench, yelling and pointing. This goes on for two more pitches until the third-base umpire sits him down with a warning. I'm ex-hausted, the Twins are finished, and Reggie has climbed a beanball onto the front page once again.

Tuesday, May 6. The Yankees dealt me my first bitter loss of the season tonight, when Bucky Dent hit a ninth-inning homer to beat the Milwaukee Brewers. The margin of victory was one run, which was exactly what the Brewers lost in the fifth inning on a fan interference call. With three runs already in, no outs and Sal Bando on second, Sixto Lezcano lifted a fly down the rightfield line. Bobby Brown raced over to catch the ball and Bando tagged up to go to third after the catch. But no, Brown dropped the ball, and the umpire ruled that a fan had reached onto the playing field and interfered. The batter was out and Bando had to return to second. The next batter's fly to left would have scored a runner from third, but with Bando on second it was useless. And speaking of useless, Gorman Thomas made the third out and Bando never scored.

Frank Messer said the umpire's call was good common sense, but it seemed dreadfully unfair to me—especially when the TV camera returned to the spot of the foul and we saw a Milwaukee usher in discussion with a fan wearing a Yankee jacket and Yankee helmet. Of course, we know how the Yankee management tries to control fan interference in its own park, thanks to last year's famous Andy Biengardo incident. With two outs in the second inning and the California Angels at bat, Yankee first baseman Chris Chambliss chased a foul popup to the stands behind first base. Chambliss leaned in and was about to catch the ball when the 19-year-old Biengardo, trying for a souvenir, touched the ball first. The Yankees asked for an interference call, but the umpire said no because the ball was in the seats and the fans were within their rights. Yankee management, however, followed a different logic: security personnel removed Andy from his box seat, held him in the security director's office for four innings, then kicked him out of the Stadium, without a refund. The security director's explanation: "The kid was ejected partially for his own safety"—i.e., to protect him from the infuriated fans around him who accused Andy of being a California fan. This didn't explain the other reasons for the ejection, or why security thought Andy would be any safer sitting in a parking lot in the Bronx waiting for his ride back to Newburgh, New York.

Wednesday, May 7. It's a downer to come home after an evening with friends, turn on the TV at quarter of eleven and see Tommy John still on the mound for the Yankees. I got to watch three swings by Brewer batters—ground-ball single, fly out and 6–4–3 doubleplay—and the game was over. John is the only Yankee to pitch a complete game so far this year, and he now has three.

Bucky Dent's home run last night, it turns out, was his first game-winning home run since October 2, 1978. You remember that one, don't you?—a fatal fly that landed on the leftfield screen of Boston's Fenway Park in the sudden-death American League Eastern Division playoff, the greatest nine-inning baseball game of the 1970s. That home run by Dent was one of the bitterest pills any Yankee-hater has ever had to swallow, not just because it was the turning point of the game or because it wouldn't have been a home run in Yankee Stadium or most other ballparks. It was sickening because if there was one person in that Yankee lineup who shouldn't beat you with a home run, it was Bucky Dent. Bucky Dent shouldn't even get a hit when a major league pitcher is bearing down in a clutch situation. Dent is a solid number nine hitter. When Billy Martin drew the lineup out of a hat in 1977, Dent was still number nine, which told you both how solid a number-nine hitter Billy considered Dent and how honest Billy's lottery was. Everything else in that Yankee–Red Sox playoff was a fitting climax to the dramatic month that had gone before. The pitchers, the fielders, the hitters that had gotten the two teams this far did their respective things. Dent's home run was the aberration, the wild card, the disaster that should have, and could have, been avoided.

The game was so good that New York's Channel 11 re-broadcast it in its entirety one month before the 1979 season began. I couldn't leave the set for a minute, and knowing the outcome only slightly lessened the suspense. The second time around I could watch with a more analytical eye, looking, always, to answer the question, could the Red Sox really have won? Without Dent's home run—or even better, if Yaz had doubled in the ninth—I would not have had the opportunity to root against the Yankees in the Playoffs against Kansas City or the Dodgers in the World Series. At the time, however, I was willing to make that sacrifice.

Saturday, May 10. If his performance on the field exaggerated the Saga of the Beanball into melodrama, Reggie's comments in the days that followed practically turned the issue into another hostage crisis. On the sidelines with a pulled thigh muscle (of unrelated origin), his only means of dominating the news was his mouth, which is all he needs.

On Day 1 Jackson indicated the gravity of the affair: "It's an ugly part of baseball. But it has to be dealt with. There's no law, there's no justice." By Day 5 Reggie felt he had to tighten the screws: "I will protect my domain. I will jeopardize the team's chances and everybody else's. I'd try to take someone's life literally in my own hands. I'd do everything I could to retaliate." To continue the analogy, there are clues that his threats are as much for domestic consumption as for their effect on the enemy pitching staff: "It seems they knock down black ballplayers more than they do white ballplayers. It's hard for me to make that statement. I won't get any sympathy for saying that." (There's Reggie, reminding us of the disadvantages he has overcome, while remaining a man who will say what he believes no matter how unpopular it is.) And later: "You're not going to intimidate a good hitter, a guy like me who has hit 375 home runs." (A little self-promotion from a man who has his lifetime statistics in his head.)

Unfortunately, Reggie didn't recover in time to face Koosman Friday night when the Twins came to town for a return three-game series. The Yankees' 5–2 win, with the unflamboyant Bob Watson getting all five RBIs, was, as a result, anticlimactic. One measure of exactly how unflamboyant Watson is is that he thought Jackson was going to pinch-hit for him in the eighth. "I wouldn't have minded," Watson said, "I'm not too proud."

Reggie saved his return for tonight, when he got to face

Darrell Jackson. Jackson *le jeune* had allegedly knocked Reggie down a week before, setting up the Koosman incident the following day. Worse, this fellow alumnus of Arizona State had taunted Reggie throughout the Koosman affair. "It's bush, but he is a kid," said Reggie after that game. "He clapped his approval when I went down. He is too small of a man, too little, to ridicule me."

Not too small, however, to shut out the Yankees for ten innings en route to a 1–0 win. Reggie went 0-for-3 before leaving the game for, I suspect, defensive reasons. His main contribution had been to let a pop fly bounce off his leg for a double. I couldn't tell whether it was because he couldn't run, couldn't see or couldn't bend over, but it apparently made Howser nervous to have him out there in the late stages of a scoreless game.

The Yankees would have gotten that one run first, and Underwood would have had a two-hour shutout win, but for the game's key play: in the bottom of the seventh with runners on first and third and one out, Piniella hit a slow twisting grounder to first. The throw to second got one out, and there was no chance for a doubleplay. But Yankee DH Eric Soderholm barreled into the shortstop just to make sure. Since the shortstop was already five feet out of the basepath, however, the umpire pumped his arm twice for an automatic doubleplay. See, Reggie? There is justice in baseball and violence does not pay.

Sunday, May 11. A 2:01 Tommy John special in the rain today, 1–0 over the hapless Twins. The Yankees' seven wins in eight games have quietly lifted them into first place, tied with the pretender Blue Jays. The rise has been quiet due to New York's new pitching rotation of Guidry, John and Underwood: all are lefthanders, all work quickly and all throw strikes. Games proceed at a two-hour pace and are decided with one rally. They are like shootouts in which the gunfighters use silencers.

Maybe the Twins are a special case: they have no right-handed power and until yesterday had not won a game against a lefthanded starter. One run in eleven innings off Underwood and May hardly constitutes breaking out of that slump, either. As for John, he has a history of being unbeatable in the first half of the season, then tailing off after the All-Star Game. So I am not too concerned by the fact that he already has six wins while no other Yankee pitcher has more than two. What does bother me is that the All-Star Game is still two months away.

Tuesday, May 13. The Kansas City Royals actually started a righthanded pitcher against the Yankees tonight, the first time in two weeks a team has done that. Next surprise: he gave up only one hit in six innings and the Royals won, 4–1. Conventional wisdom is to throw lefties at the Yanks to thwart their lefthanded power: Jackson, Nettles, Gamble, Spencer. When Rivers and Chambliss were fixtures in the lineup last year, the imbalance was even greater. As a result, the pitchers with reputations as Yankee-killers today are lefties like Caldwell of the Brewers and Gura and Splittorff of the Royals. In fact, Splittorff was supposed to be the eleventh lefty in a row to face the Yankees tonight, and the twenty-first in the last twenty-five games, but a bad back in warm-ups threw the start to an obscure second-year relief pitcher named Renie Martin.

Yankee teams have always had and will continue to have lefthanded power because of the shape of Yankee Stadium. Modern symmetrical stadiums, like Baltimore's, tend to produce more balanced teams. But the rightfield foul line in old Yankee Stadium was a famous 296 feet and is still only 310. Just as important, the stands don't curve back from the foul pole in right as sharply as they do in left. Left-center in Yankee Stadium (430 feet) is known as Death Valley in honor of the many drives by righthanded sluggers that have died there. A fly to right need only be pulled to have a chance of leaving the playing field. Maybe the westerly winds have something to do with it, too. Whatever the cause, the evidence is overwhelming. Ruth and Gehrig. Berra and Mize. Mantle and Maris. Jackson and Nettles.

Boston's Fenway Park is the opposite: the Green Monster can turn a routine fly to left into a home run. Hobson, Rice, Evans, Perez, Fisk—the Red Sox load up on righthanded sluggers, and conventional wisdom says it's suicide to pitch a lefty against Boston. Mel Parnell is a legend for winning twenty games in Fenway. Three years ago the Yankees acquired Dave Kingman just to play one series there.

Reinforcing conventional wisdom these days is the American League schedule. The Western Division teams play Boston and New York back-to-back. So if you're a manager and have pitchers of both persuasions, you use the righties in Boston and save the southpaws for the Yankees. So what if the Yankees don't seem to be having any trouble beating lefties this year. You won't get fired for being conventional.

Wednesday, May 14. I turned on Phil and Fran while doing the dishes tonight. After two convincing wins in Yankee Stadium, 12–3 and 4–1, the Royals were battling the law of averages as well as the Yankees, and I didn't hold out much hope for them. That "much" dropped to "any" when I heard that Guidry was on the mound. So I decided to spend the evening catching up on some writing and reading. Just out of curiosity I turned the radio back on two hours later. The Yankees were leading 14–2. Things were so well in hand that they had brought in Ed Figueroa to pitch.

One of the things I was catching up on was Roger Angell's quarterly baseball piece in the *New Yorker,* this one about spring training. In the last decade there have been two serious baseball writers who have given as much status to the game as they have received themselves through their writings. Because they both are named Roger, and because their seminal works were both published in 1972 and contained the word *Summer* in their titles, there was much confusion among the baseball-reading public as to which author wrote which book. From continuing to read their work, and because they are actually very different writers, I eventually learned the difference.

Roger Angell writes understated, calmly analytic essay-length pieces that are invariably published in the *New Yorker* a month or two after the events they describe and are sometimes collected in book form, as in *The Summer Game.* The game of baseball achieves an importance in his work not because of any claims he makes for it, but because he writes about it with a seriousness befitting a study of the SALT talks or the world's leading philosopher-mathematician, which is what the *New Yorker* carries in the same space when Angell is not writing. His greatest accomplishment is the way his measured prose captures the rhythm, the pace, of a normal baseball game. Along the way are small points that do not turn into runs but contribute to the season statistics, and there are larger points that do register on the scoreboard. At the end, we can tote up the runs and find the winner, the overriding theme; but more importantly, we find lingering in our minds the sights and sounds of the ballpark on the slow sunny afternoon or the crisp clear evening, the relief from having totally left the outside world for three hours to inhabit a smaller world where everything can be known and appreciated, where we can experience pleasure and agony without ever being threatened in our personal lives. When the occasion merits it, Angell can also capture the drama of baseball, as he did in his most memorable piece, called "Agincourt and After," which described the Cincinnati-Boston World Series of 1975, above all the great sixth game won by Carlton Fisk's home run.

For Roger Kahn, author of *The Boys of Summer,* everything is drama, and usually very serious drama at that. The game is not just a game, but a metaphor for life. We are never far from a message. The contrast between these two writers is apparent in their styles. Angell's stock-in-trade is the five-comma sentence. There is usually a clause of explanation and a clause of history that is more important than the verb. As in: "The umpires, who were on strike for higher wages last spring, worked the spring games as usual this year, but some of them appeared to be feeling a mite irritable for the preseason, when games are customarily conducted in a lighthearted, almost offhand fashion." Or the sentence before that one, a sentence that happens to summarize Angell's baseball philosophy: "As Dave Garcia pointed out, one of the wonders of baseball is that every aspect of the game is visible, but another wonder, I know now, is how much of it we can watch, summer after summer, and never see at all." Where Angell's sentences are languid and lazy, Kahn's are short, choppy, and dripping with drama. Take this passage from his short-lived column for *Time* Magazine. It appeared in 1977, but is still timely this week before the strike: "I had been traveling. Boston. Minneapolis. Pittsburgh. Toronto. Fort Worth. The landscape and the weather and the accents changed. The theme of the questions persisted. Money." In another column he joins some middle-aged businessman at a hockey camp. The experience is part of a search for something bigger: "On a warm August night, in a southern Ontario town called Guelph, a dozen Americans are playing hockey. There are no commercial interruptions. There is no crowd." And finally, the piece concludes: "We begin, George and I, to define sport."

When he is writing about a small subject, like a hockey camp for middle-aged men, Kahn's portentousness sounds overdrawn and a bit absurd. His prose works beautifully, however, when the subject is monumental. And there are few baseball stories more monumental than the 1950s Brooklyn Dodgers, the subject of *The Boys of Summer*. Kahn's book, of course, is about something bigger than the games played on the field: "But I mean to be less concerned with curve balls than with the lure of the team." And with what happened to them after they left baseball, as a way to magnify even larger the memory of, the nostalgia for, one of the most famous teams ever to play the game.

The Brooklyn Dodgers of 1952–53, the years Kahn covered them for the *Herald Tribune,* were my first favorite team. Perhaps it was because they took on the Yankees in the World Series those years. Growing up around New York I had, theoretically, three choices, but I had only one friend who rooted for the Giants. The fact that I remember his predilection twenty-five years later shows how unusual that was. The rest of us chose between the Yankees and the Dodgers. Though they were in different leagues, there was no way you could root for both. I of course wasn't around for the Dodgers' lean years, when the Brooklyn "Bums" established a reputation such as the Mets would have in their first six years. When I came of rooting age, the Dodgers were the second-best team in baseball, and it struck me as one of the great anomalies of history that they had never won a World Series, thanks mainly to the New York Yankees. In my youthful opinion, Duke Snider was a better centerfielder than Mickey Mantle, and I felt the same way, though slightly less strongly, about the relative merits of Reese and Rizzuto, Campanella and Berra, Furillo and Bauer and on down the line. By always winning, the Yankees were boring and distant, as hard to identify with as a school principal. By never quite winning—with the glorious exception of 1955 when Johnny Podres shut out the Yankees in the seventh game—the Dodgers were a team you could root for, feel sorry for, pray for and be proud of. No one ever would have forgotten that team anyway, but Roger Kahn created a fitting memorial. By comparing Jackie Robinson to *Brown* v. *Board of Education,* Kahn invests the legend with dimensions far broader than the confines of Ebbets Field. Still, if there is a baseball team that can support Kahn's Homeric treatment, the Brooklyn Dodgers were it. The name itself has already passed into history and, unlike the Washington Senators, will never return.

Between Kahn's and Angell's two views of baseball, one macro, the other micro, I prefer the latter. But that is hardly what matters. Instead, it is that they have given the game, my game, such scholarly attention, and lifted it from the sports pages to a higher realm of thought and expression.

Friday, May 16. Tommy John stretched his record to 7–0 tonight. The Rangers didn't knock him out early, when he was vulnerable, and he just got better. I missed most of the game, but for the ten minutes I listened, I got to hear the latest Reggie Jackson story, as revealed by Phil Rizzuto:

"You know, that Reggie just does so much that nobody hears about. I hope Reggie doesn't get mad at me; I don't know whether he wants anybody to mention it. But I saw Officer C——— before the game and he told me that Reggie bought six bulletproof vests for the police force. They cover the front *and* the back and those things cost a lot of money. And you know, Reggie specified that one should go to Officer C———, who he knows is always on duty at the Stadium. And what's more, this one has across the front a big number 44!"

Right, Phil. Reggie was probably trying to keep that one quiet.

Chapter 3
THE YANKEES MOVE INTO FIRST PLACE
Beating Up on the Weak Sisters

Saturday, May 17. Joined to the trend of single games on Sunday afternoon is the rise of Saturday Night Baseball Fever. Saturday afternoon games in New York are historically low-attendance affairs, and Steinbrenner and his fellow owners no doubt figured that they could improve box office receipts by moving the games to the evenings. Of course, I am opposed to this on all the traditional grounds, as well as on the grounds of tradition. But it does mean there is less competition on the tube Saturday afternoon for NBC's Game of the Week, and today's offering was tempting on two counts. It was my first chance to see Billy Martin in an Oakland uniform and to see the Yankees' current challengers for first place in the American League East, the Toronto Blue Jays.

It was a daring pairing for national TV, and NBC's first game ever from Canada. Last year these two teams had the worst records in the majors, losing a remarkable 217 games between them. The seventh-place Blue Jays finished 28½ games behind the Indians, not to mention 50½ games behind the Orioles. This year, however, both teams have been at the top of their divisions, so they must be playing some kind of exciting baseball, right? Wrong. If there are two teams that are less offensive than Joe Namath's Brut commercial, it's the A's and the Jays. Martin's disrespect for the Blue Jay bats was so great that he left his obviously tired starter, Matt Keough, in the game for fourteen innings, which is how long it took for Oakland to score a third run to win the game. The night before, these two teams produced a total of one run.

Billy looked mean, vicious, genuinely unhappy the entire game. If the young A's are playing well, it has got to be out of fear. Billy had a birthday the day before, but at 52 he is still not too old to yell at players half his age. In fairness to Billy, he also picked on 43-year-old Clete Boyer, the only Yankee of the early '60s I liked, perhaps because he was the only Yankee on that team who couldn't hit. Being a great third baseman, however, does not necessarily make one a great third-base coach. Boyer started to wave in, then held up, a runner who would have scored because the throw from the outfield skipped past the relay man. The runner never scored, and when Boyer got back to the dugout, one of the game's great second-guessers let him have it. It's one of those management techniques that so endeared Billy to me when he was in New York.

Tuesday, May 20. The announcers' two favorite observations during the early innings of tonight's game in Detroit were (1) that Yankee starter Tommy John had not given up a home run all year, and (2) that Tiger power hitter (or so he had been billed by the Mets, his previous team) Richie Hebner had not hit a home run all year. When Hebner unloaded with a two-out grand slam in the next inning, it turned around a ball game and, just perhaps, the Yankee season.

Through 4⅔ innings John was coasting along, on his way to an 8–0 record and his 200th lifetime win. Guidry had won 1–0 the night before, and it was becoming apparent that good years from Guidry and John might be enough to propel the Yankees to the pennant, with only average years from the rest of the team. In the Yankee starting lineup Ruppert Jones was hitting .221, Lou Piniella .194, Graig Nettles .242, Bucky Dent .233, and Rick Cerone .202. Bob Watson, at .306, was the only regular over .275. Guidry and John between them, however, had a combined 11–0 record. Without them, the Yankees were 9–13, but with them they had built a four-game lead over Boston, Milwaukee, and Baltimore.

Then, after a two-out walk to Kemp and a single by Parrish, John bounced a wild pitch past Cerone, and the 31,000 fans sensed that John had lost control of the game. Wockenfuss walked and Hebner, with a wristless, rusty-gate swing, pulled the ball down the line and into the rightfield stands. The Tigers wound up scoring twelve earned runs off John, Davis and Gossage—a hopeful harbinger, indeed.

Friday, May 23. Just a quick note of relief that there will not be a baseball strike today. Haven't heard any details yet, so I remain in emotional limbo regarding the terms of the settlement between the players and owners.

The key issue was free-agent compensation, and the players had the following arguments on their side:

• They've got it: Free agency, as the result of an arbitrator's decision subsequently upheld by the courts, exists and the players have it. The owners want the players to give it up but have offered nothing in return.

• They deserve it: To be eligible, a player must first make the majors, then stay there for six years. He must play out the option year on his contract, which means foregoing a pay raise for one year and giving up all security and much fan support. And if he has a bad year or gets hurt, he will lose the gamble.

• It has helped the owners: Since free agency began, attendance at ballparks has steadily risen, and TV revenues have increased as well. The year-round publicity generated by free-agent activity has kept baseball on the sports pages through the winter and has been a notable part of baseball's resurgence as the national pastime.

• It has helped baseball: Rather than become less competitive, baseball has become more competitive thanks to free agency. A team can turn around its fortunes without waiting five years for the farm clubs to develop new talent. At the same time, teams without free agents—Cincinnati, Kansas City, Baltimore—have shown that you don't have to sign free agents to produce a winner.

• It's the American way: Free agency is nothing more than the rule of the marketplace that applies in every other American industry. CBS didn't have to offer even a draft pick yesterday when it signed Pillsbury's vice-chairman Tom Wyman to a three-year contract worth more than $3.4 million—a better deal than Nolan Ryan got.

The owners' only argument seems to be that because of free agency they have to pay salaries that are financially ruinous. This argument is undercut by the fact that it is the owners themselves who are pushing salaries to levels never dreamed of by the players, and also by the fact that they will not divulge financial statements to support their argument. Finally, the owners are independently wealthy from other businesses, while the players are in the game for their bread and butter. If any owner can't take the financial strain, it's very easy to sell. Just look at the bidding last winter for the cellar-dwelling Mets. The owners' attitude was not designed to win much sympathy, either: late to meetings, no comments allowed to press, intransigence all around. And for a spokesman they picked Ray Grebey, who was surly, argumentative, incommunicative and ungracious when NBC's Bryant Gumbel, hardly a firebrand, tried to interview him during last Saturday's Game of the Week.

The surprise is that with all the arguments favoring the players, the fan in the street was not supporting the players. If Harris or Yankelovich had taken a poll, I bet you would

have found 40 percent hoping to see the players get a come-
uppance and another 40 percent saying a plague on both
their houses.

Saturday, May 24. On a softball field in Central Park, I finally
ran into the man who bet me five dollars last year that Ron
Guidry would win more games than Dennis Eckersley. Actually, I was the one who forced the bet on him, and it was
a follow-up to our more complicated bet in 1978 that Eckersley and Mike Torrez would win more games for the Red Sox
than any two Yankee pitchers. Eckersley was a favorite of
mine from his three seasons at Cleveland, when he practically
had to pitch a no-hitter, which he did once, to be assured of
winning. Cleveland was the first team in my sports lifetime
to beat the Yankees, and I have rooted for the Indians in
gratitude ever since. And although I have received little rec-
ompense for this choice since 1954, the Indians have generally managed to produce one pitcher—Herb Score, Cal Mc-
Lish, Sam McDowell, Gaylord Perry, Eckersley—whom I
could root for with some likelihood of success, no matter how
badly the rest of the team was doing. With the Red Sox' hitting
behind him, Eckersley was a sure 20-game winner. That's
exactly what he won, but Guidry had his phenomenal 25–3
season, and the surprising Tommy John added 21 wins, five
more than Torrez.

In '79 I knew Guidry couldn't repeat his previous success and I thought Eckersley would. For half the season I
had a lock on the five dollars. Guidry volunteered for bullpen
duty after Gossage sprained his thumb and Eckersley built
up a five-win lead. Then in August Eckersley started to come
up empty and Guidry began an eight-game winning streak.
For me the tension climaxed on September 3 when the Yankees, by this time fourteen and one-half games behind Baltimore, faced off against the Sox for a three-game series, and
Eckersley and Guidry were named the starting pitchers.

As I turned on the radio to listen, I knew in my gut that Eckersley would not pull it off—and when he was knocked out in the second inning, I consoled myself that he'd at least get plenty of rest before his next start. My hopes were then pinned on Guidry's not getting the win, and they were still alive when Boston narrowed New York's lead to 6–5 in the top of the eighth and knocked out Guidry. I made a deal with the Radio Devil, one of the few superstitious forces in my life: let the Red Sox score again and I will agree to let the Yankees ultimately win the game. The deal went through all right, but I had left a large loophole. The Red Sox scored their sixth run in the ninth—but only after the Yankees had added four insurance runs in the bottom of the eighth. Guidry picked up the win, which provided his season margin of one over Eckersley.

By the time the season ended, however, the Yankee fan I bet with had switched jobs. It is probably just as well that we didn't meet again until this week. By then only a fool would have bet a third time against Guidry, or John. As if to confirm this analysis, Guidry improved his record to 5–0 last night. This time when I turned on the radio and heard Willie Randolph homer to lead off the game and the Yankees take a 3–0 lead in the first inning, I didn't even bother to call on the Radio Devil. With the Yankees playing Toronto, I had no chips to negotiate with.

Sunday, May 25. It's the Memorial Day weekend and the Yankees are cruising along in first place, winning games at a .632 clip. The top story of the Yankee season so far—Guidry and John—is no surprise. But the second key development, one that is just becoming obvious, is the unexpected emergence of the Yankee rookies. The Yankees by tradition are a veteran team. Every now and then a player will earn a transient spot on the squad through a good showing in spring training, but more common are the Gordon Windhorns, who win the James

P. Dawson Award as top rookie in camp and then have a Yankee career that lasts all of eleven at-bats. The only rookie nonpitcher to stick with the Yankees in the last *ten* years is Willie Randolph, and he arrived at spring training in 1976 with 30 games for Pittsburgh under his belt.

I was surprised that any rookies made the 25-man roster this year. When three made it, I suspected that the Yankees mainly wanted three fewer players pulling down six-figure salaries while complaining about not getting to play. To my surprise, not only has Dick Howser begun to give his rookies regular work, but last week, in the wake of Oscar Gamble's foot injury, he added a fourth to the team. On Thursday night Mike Griffin pitched his first major league win, rightfielder Joe Lefebvre homered in his first major league game, and leftfielder Bobby Brown went 2-for-4 to raise his season average to .300. The other rookie, Dennis Werth, is hitting .500 in his limited role as righthanded pinch hitter and hit his first home run Friday night. Howser, up from college coaching, may actually be good at bringing along young players. It is probably no coincidence that the two biggest nights for the rookies were games away from New York against Toronto, the weakest team in the division, the night before and the night after the threatened player strike, when more attention was focused away from the playing field than on it.

"Lefebvre, meanwhile, left the ballpark with a special souvenir. His home run ball was retrieved by an usher and suitably inscribed by Reggie Jackson, who said Catfish Hunter had done the same for him when he was a Kansas City A's rookie in 1967." (*New York Post*). Lefebvre, who homered the next night in his second major league game for an American League record, may find it easier to get Reggie out of rightfield than out of the newspapers. Just as nature fills a vacuum, Reggie fills a spotlight. Not only did Reggie find a way to join in the rookie's big moment, he managed to drop Catfish Hunter's name in the process, bathing himself with some more reflected greatness. (If Hunter did in fact sign that ball for Reggie, it was undoubtedly in jest. Hunter's lifetime record at that point was a far-from-Cooperstown 30 wins and 38 losses.)

Reggie, of course, has used less defenseless props than Lefebvre as stepping stools to the spotlight. When Carl Yastrzemski got the 3,000th hit of his nineteen-year major league career on national TV against the Yankees last September, who was the first Yankee on the scene, giving Yaz a bear hug? Reggie Jackson, it was widely noted, had even gone to Fenway Park two nights before on an off-day for the Yankees, to watch Yaz make his first try for 3,000. It was widely noted, of course, because Jackson watched the game from the press box. Jackson, no doubt, wanted to watch that historic moment. But Jackson can't just watch a historic moment, he has to make himself part of it. Through the implications of his actions, he let everybody know that he could relate in a special way to Yaz, that the two of them were superstar soulmates, that it was only some historic accident that Yaz was going for 3,000 hits, not Reggie, that both are, indeed, great men, slotted for adjacent lockers in baseball heaven. The last, I must interject, rates a loud "No way" if we're talking about the Hall of Fame: Yaz is a shoo-in; Reggie has a decade of sportswriters' scorn and bemusement to overcome.

The Reggie-Yaz incident was merely a warm-up, however, for Reggie's biggest scene of 1979, six days later. Catfish Hunter was retiring from baseball, albeit a year too late, the Yankees were honoring him with a "Day," and Reggie asked to present his own gift to his former Oakland teammate. No one else in baseball, it is safe to say, would have tried to use another player's "Day" to make a personal presentation. It was a perfect display of the Reggie Jackson paradox, the two sides of his character meshing as smoothly as the horsehide strips of a baseball. The giving, generous side of Reggie was there in his desire to honor his friend. The self-displaying, egotistical side was there in his choice of where and when to do it: in Yankee Stadium in full view of the fans and the TV cameras. Just as Reggie was on hand to celebrate Yaz's 3,000th hit, just as he autographed the baseball for young Lefebvre's home run, and just as he was on the front line and front page as Yankee player rep during last week's strike showdown, Reggie wanted to be there for Hunter's last moment, to join in the glory surrounding one of the great pitchers of the 1970s.

Yankee management said no, Reggie blasted George Steinbrenner, and George in turn savaged Reggie, complaining not only about Reggie's ego but about his missing a payment on a previously undisclosed personal loan. That just about severed Reggie's famous friendship with George for all time, if you could believe Reggie's reported reaction. Catfish Hunter got to keep his day for himself, but Reggie ended up with the headlines. I hope he at least gave Catfish the gift. I don't know what it was, but I suspect it had a number 44 on it somewhere.

Tuesday, May 27. Guess what teams are in first place this morning? The Dodgers, the Phillies, the Royals and the Yankees. Sounds like 1978, not to mention 1977, all over again. Of the four, the team with the biggest lead and the one I am most worried about is the Yankees. They manhandled the Tigers yesterday, 13–5, after taking three of four games from the Blue Jays. They get to play Toronto again next weekend, then the bulk of their June schedule is a home-and-away set against the three West Coast teams. If Oakland and Seattle are as soft as they look and if the California Angels continue their season-long slump, New York's lead could be pretty sizable before the Yankees even have to look at the Boston Red Sox come June 23.

Wednesday, May 28. My one surprise in last night's 9–6 win over the Tigers was seeing an unfamiliar Yankee come to the plate in the first inning and proceed to dig a hole with his back foot in the batter's box. Who is this guy batting third in front of Reggie Jackson and acting like he owns the place?

Number 46 turned out to be rookie phee-nom Joe Lefebvre, hitting .571 after one week in the majors. He didn't show much at the plate last night, but he played rightfield in Yankee Stadium with a quickness and aplomb I haven't seen there since Reggie arrived.

This kid not only wants to play and knows how to play, he is going to get the chance. Centerfielder Ruppert Jones went under the knife without advance notice yesterday to remove an intestinal obstruction. The loss of Jones puts off the tough question of who goes down when Gamble returns, and it will give the Yankees a long look at Bobby Brown, the 26-year-old almost-rookie switch-hitter who will start in Jones's place. It is possible that the Yankee outfield of the next generation is evolving before our eyes. And it is possible that the next generation will be here as soon as next year. Piniella is 36 and not hitting; Reggie, 34, still can't field and is injury-prone; Murcer, 34, is as good as gone; Gamble, 30, is suited for the pinch-hitter/DH role; White, 36, hit a game-winning homer yesterday, but it was in Tokyo. Brown, Jones and Lefebvre are 26, 25 and 24 and can run the basepaths and field their positions. Whether they can win pennants is something we may know more about by October.

Thursday, May 29. I anxiously awaited the 7:30 radio news this morning, eager for validation. There it was: Detroit beat the Yankees last night, 6–3. I had been at the ballpark and seen the Yankees go down to defeat in person, but somehow I couldn't be sure it would count in the standings until I heard it on the radio and read it in the newspaper. It's one of those confusions of illusion and reality that infects our society. Once, they say, *seeing* was believing; nowadays, hearing Warner Wolf or reading the *Times* is when you believe.

This news was, in fact, somewhat incredible. The lowly Tigers, who had looked like amateurs in a beer commercial the night before, had dealt Ron Guidry his first loss of the year and only the second loss in his last eighteen decisions. It happened rather quietly, too. Brookens singled and Stegman homered in the second. Then in the sixth, five singles, a sacrifice fly, and a throwing error by Guidry produced four more runs and a 6-0 lead. Guidry never seemed to falter or lose control, and he pitched his fourth 1-2-3 inning in the seventh before departing in favor of May and Gossage. It was, as he commented afterward, just one of those outings when the law of averages catches up to you.

The other news, for me, came before the game, when I got to see the Yankees' new warm-up T-shirts. I have always felt a grudging respect for the Yankee pinstripe uniform at the same time that I have loathed the coldly efficient, corporate image it symbolized. In the days when most baseball uniforms looked the same, differentiated by the name across the chest or the animal on the sleeve, the Yankee pinstripe was unique, another reflection of Yankee arrogance. They didn't need the word "Yankees" spelled out in script letters like the Dodgers or block letters like the Giants. Anybody who was anybody, the uniform seemed to say, knew what the pinstripe meant. And how appropriate, too, the pinstripe trademark was for New York, the financial capital of the world. But whoever heard of rooting for the Chase Manhattan Bank?

I might be glad the Yankees were in New York, just as I was glad that the big banks are here, for the sake of New York's prestige around the world, but I considered myself too much of a free spirit to root for people in pinstripes.

Charlie Finley succeeded in destroying most of the traditions that went with uniforms when he dressed his Oakland A's in green and gold doubleknit outfits, followed by old teams like the Pittsburgh Pirates, who redesigned the baseball cap, and new teams like the Houston Astros, who for some reason stuck rainbows on their jerseys. The Yankees switched to doubleknit, too, but resisted another trend by leaving their names off their backs. Now, for no good reason that I can see, the Yankees put on a different uniform when they warm up before the game: on top of their pinstripe pants they wear dark blue, almost black T-shirts with their uniform number in big block white on the back. If they are looking to be more with-it, they have succeeded, for these shirts are just the thing that would be worn by Imperial Storm Troopers, if they had a baseball team. But on a scale of lovability, I suspect that even David Rockefeller outranks Darth Vader.

Friday, May 30. The worst thing about the renovation of Yankee Stadium in 1975 was its cost, which has passed from the pages of the *Village Voice* into accepted folklore as being in the neighborhood of $110 million. The second worst thing was the "modern" scoreboard that was installed. I put that word in quotes because, while the scoreboard was completely electronic and was supposed to represent a great advance in technology, it really constituted a giant step backward in everything having to do with baseball.

First, it had no section for out-of-town scores. The old Yankee Stadium scoreboard showed what half-inning was being played, what the score was at the start of that half-inning, and who was pitching. Reading this part of the scoreboard was, for the sophisticated fan, a dramatic art. "Oooh, the White Sox have changed pitchers, Boston must have a rally going." "Gee, it's been the bottom of the sixth in Baltimore for the last twenty minutes, must be a big inning." Whoever ordered the million-dollar Yankee scoreboard was apparently not a sophisticated baseball fan, however, for this section was eliminated. Instead, the scores would be flashed on the message board two or three times a night. That was it. No continuing drama in the wings. No chance to impress your neighbors by being the first to spot a new score. No chance for the mental calculations: if the Yankees lose this one and the Red Sox can hold on to win in Boston and the Orioles can just get two runs in the ninth, then . . .

Less important was dropping the player lineups, which you could figure out yourself as the game went along. But there was no way, if you missed the pregame introductions, you were going to find out who the umpires were, so that you could personalize your epithets. That information, too, used to be a fixture on the old scoreboard.

What did we get instead? We got an electronic message board used only for welcoming the Elks Lodge from Whippany, N.J., and promoting Bat Day. Plus the supposed main attraction, a replay screen that was used to show Yankee home runs and made them look like impressionist paintings viewed from the distance of one foot. While umpires were lodging protests against other clubs who used replay screens to show them up on controversial calls, none complained about the Monet Water Lilies shown by the Yankees.

After a year or two of fan protests, including my letter to Gabe Paul—so far my only communication with Yankee management—the Yankees added an auxiliary scoreboard on which out-of-town scores could be flashed more regularly. There is still no permanent display, and gone forever is the magic moment when the previous score is taken down—manually, by a real human being—and the crowd holds its breath in anticipation of what the new score will be. And I can't remember the replay screen's being used once at Wednesday night's game with the Tigers, except for the shots of Guidry standing on the mound and the flag waving in air during the singing of "The Star-Spangled Banner." Of course, outside of Murcer's late home run, there really wasn't much that the Yankee fans wanted to see a second time.

The scoreboard was put to one good use that night, however. In the second inning it announced that the Yankees had signed centerfielder Paul Blair to take the injured Ruppert Jones's place on the roster. The 26,000 fans greeted this news with a warm hand and, after recovering from my surprise, I joined in. I immediately remembered one time before when I had rooted for Blair as a Yankee. It was in the ninth inning of the fifth game of the Playoffs in Kansas City in 1977, and I have never so badly wanted the Yankees to lose a game. They had broken the Royals' hearts on Chris Chambliss's home run in the same situation the year before. And they were just finishing the ugliest season of personality conflicts on a baseball team in modern times, the season that Reggie Jackson arrived as the straw to stir the Yankees into the drink. But Blair wasn't a part of that. First, he had been an Oriole, playing against the Yankees, for thirteen years. He was a defensive specialist, not an offensive prima donna, and he had done whatever Martin asked him, without complaint: pinch-run, fill in for injured infielders, play outfield in the late innings. Most important in this Playoff situation, he was playing in place of the *benched* Reggie Jackson. Benching Reggie in the season's biggest game was the best thing that had happened all year, but if his replacement did poorly, Reggie would have the last word. So I found myself rooting for Blair. And I felt like the boy who took his finger out of the dike when Blair not only singled but scored the tying run and sparked the Yankee rally that won the game, 4–3, and put the Yankees into the World Series.

I rooted for Blair again last season when the Yankees cut him and Cincinnati picked him up. But at 36, and now with a job as a Yankee instructor (one of his assignments this spring was teaching Reggie how to play the outfield), Blair, I've decided, no longer needs my support. So I salute him for his character and his former grace afield, and I applaud the Yankees for showing him this respect and for actually using their scoreboard to give us some baseball news. But when Paul Blair gets in his next game, he won't find me making any more exceptions. I will treat him as just another Yankee.

Monday, June 2. Ugh. Two weeks—13 straight games—against Toronto and Detroit has got to be the pits. The Yankees won 10 of those games and had the most successful month of May for any Yankee team since 1958. They are in first place by 4½ games and own a .644 winning percentage, highest by far in the majors. They have been able to give important playing time to four rookies and they have let their new catcher start every single game and overcome his very shaky start.

The weakness of the opposition has disguised the fact that the Yankees, to my impartial eye, are not playing very good baseball. In the one inning I watched yesterday, which was before the Yankees scored their 11 runs, the Blue Jays scored one run on a passed ball by Cerone, a second run when Randolph dropped a ground ball and couldn't make a throw to the plate, and a third run when Dennis Werth misplayed a double in the rightfield corner and overthrew the cutoff man. And after the Yankees put the game away, Toronto got five hits and three runs in two innings off relief ace Gossage.

Hey, but the fact that the Yankees ran through Toronto three straight doesn't mean the weekend was totally dull. No, there was also a minor mutiny and an attempted murder. Unhappy to be taken out in favor of Gossage while he was pitching a three-hit shutout Friday night, Luis Tiant dropped the ball to the ground and chucked his glove into the stands. Howser put down this unprecedented rebellion swiftly and strongly, fining Tiant the maximum $500, exchanging pieces of mind with the hot-tempered Cuban hurler in the locker room, and making clear to the bloodthirsty reporters that the matter was closed. "I agree with Billy," Howser concluded, "apologies are overrated." Looking hungrily for that old player-discontent angle once again—and probably judging that everyone out there was as bored with the Blue Jays as I am —the newspapers gave the Tiant incident full headlines, completely ignoring the 6–0 game. In the month that gave us Mount St. Helens, however, I don't think that Tiant's stack-blowing rates as much of an eruption.

More a cause of wonder even than throwing a glove away—some fan returned it, presumably because it reeked so of tobacco juice that he knew his mother wouldn't let him bring it in the house—are the ways in which Reggie Jackson finds his way into the newspaper.

On his way to a fashionable Upper East Side bar for a beer after Saturday night's game-winning home run, Reggie had racial slurs and broken bottles thrown at him by the formerly anonymous Angel Viera. A couple of passersby recognized Reggie and offered to help. Then, in a rather strange move for someone whose injured leg is keeping him out of the Yankee outfield, Reggie decided to chase this guy "for the hell of it." When Angel returned and fired a gun three times in the air, hitting a sixth-floor window down the street, he was arrested and charged with attempted murder, and Reggie decided it was time for that beer after all.

Three things seemed to bother Jackson about the incident. The first, naturally, was that the guy was shooting real bullets. The second was that the press was making such a big deal of it: "I don't want to be on the front page," he said to the cluster of reporters surrounding him before Sunday's game, somewhat overestimating the attention he was to get. The third was that his assailant didn't recognize him: "Everyone else seemed to know me except this guy with the gun."

Tuesday, June 3. You listen to baseball on the radio when you're driving or doing the dishes, or are sunbathing too close to someone else's radio in the park or on the beach. Very seldom, anymore, does anyone plan time around a radio broadcast of anything, let alone a baseball game, so it is not surprising that I did not hear the announcement that routinely precedes Yankee broadcasts until last August. I had been annoyed by announcer Fran Healy for almost two years, but it was only then that I had a clue as to why Healy was on the airwaves. While Frank Messer, Bill White and "the Scooter," Phil Rizzuto, the announcement went, are employees of WPIX Channel 11, their colleague in the radio booth, Fran Healy, is employed by the New York Yankees!

There may be some perfectly innocuous explanation for this. All the announcers are obviously approved by the Yankees anyway; since Healy was needed only to bolster the radio side (when a game is televised, two of the top three handle the TV broadcast while the third, on a rotating basis, announces for radio), he couldn't very well be paid by the TV network. But other explanations were more fun—and made more sense. Did the Yankees want to keep an emergency backup catcher around? Although they never used him when he was on the roster—any more than they used such famous backup backstops as Charlie Silvera and Johnny Blanchard —Healy was an excellent defensive catcher and could probably come down from the booth and catch a game today if needed. Or maybe the Yanks signed him to a multiyear guaranteed contract when he joined them from Kansas City. If they had to pay him anyway, they might as well get some use from him by having him plug the Yankees on the radio. Making him a media personality gave them one more person they could send out to community affairs on behalf of the team, since half the players can't be counted on anymore.

But what I really think is that Fran Healy is part of Reggie Jackson's contract. Now I don't have any proof, and I probably couldn't understand Jackson's contract if I had it in front of me. And maybe Steinbrenner didn't actually put it in writing. He is always making oral deals with his players which, if you listen to them, he mostly doesn't keep. But you will remember that Healy's biggest moment in pinstripes was arranging a truce between Reggie and Billy Martin back in 1977 when each was petitioning Steinbrenner to get rid of the other —a peace-keeping mission that probably won the Yankees the pennant that year. Healy was, and for all I know still is, Jackson's best, if not only, friend on the Yankees. It's worth it for George to keep Fran around, announcing out-of-town scores, if it makes Reggie happy. And it's worth it for Reggie to have his buddy in the broadcast booth, keeping the spotlight on Reggie and keeping negative comments to a minimum. As I said, I may not be right; but if there is some explanation for Healy's being on the Yankees' payroll, it's not his abilities as a sportscaster.

My concern over Healy's status has continued to grow, because despite his tinny voice and hyper delivery, Healy's role on the air has steadily expanded. At first he merely read out-of-town scores and announcements of Yankee promotional events. Then he filled in between innings when the other announcers were switching from the TV to the radio side of the broadcast booth. Last year he began to give color comments, which White ignored, Messer tolerated, and Rizzuto thought were great. He broke into play-by-play when Rizzuto was too choked up to talk in the game after Munson's death last August, and the same thing happened early this year after a gigantic home run by Reggie took Phil's breath away.

But none of this had fully prepared me, or for that matter Healy, for tonight's game in Kansas City, when Rizzuto wasn't there at all. White started out doing the radio broadcast with Fran while Messer was left alone on the TV. The TV producer must have agreed with me that without White or Rizzuto to provoke him, Messer was excruciatingly dull —so dull that he had White leave the radio side and let Healy do three innings of play-by-play all by himself. I've never heard so many out-of-town scores in such a short period of time, but then again former catcher Healy knows that in a clutch situation you've got to go with your best pitch.

Wednesday, June 4. The Kansas City Royals beat the Yankees tonight. More than that, they whipped them, 9–3. A six-run second inning ended the contest early and gave Kansas City the series, 2–1. It is the first series the Yankees have lost since April. There is no sign yet that the Yankees won't win the Eastern Division, but at least this series gave some reassurance that in competition with the best in the league the Yankees are just another team. And although the baseball season is already nine weeks old, there are five American League teams that the Yankees have not yet played. Somewhere in that bunch may be a team that will surprise us.

Tonight's surprise was the swiftness of Kansas City's knockout punch. The Yankees scored in each of the first two innings and the Royals, with the exception of George Brett, were playing with an intensity typified by Amos Otis—who had a strike called on him while standing outside the batter's box with his bat lying on the ground. But a minute later U. L. Washington hit a line drive that took off on the Tartan-Turf for a two-out triple that tied the game, Willie Wilson singled him home, and Spencer and Randolph misplayed a grounder between them into another single. That brought up Brett, who, off his performances against the Yankees, has to be considered the best player in the American League and a surefire selection to the Yankee-Hater Hall of Fame. In the previous inning he had singled and stolen second, and in the field he made a full-speed slide to catch a foul pop. What would he do now? Only hit a three-run homer to right-center. He drove in another run in the fourth inning, again with two outs, and hustled to second base on the throw to third. Beautiful baseball!

Tiant and Figueroa gave up nine earned runs in six innings. To complete my pleasure, over on Channel 9 the man the Yankees let go, Jim Kaat, was pitching the Cardinals to a ten-inning 1–0 shutout of the Mets.

Chapter 4
THE YANKEES CALL ON
THE WEST COAST
And Find Nobody Home

Friday, June 6. Sometimes you can turn on a game for ten minutes and see practically all the action; other times, like tonight, you can watch for an hour at a time, turn your back and miss everything. I was at work, reading next week's *Time* Magazine to make sure no one got libeled, and my problem, I thought, was how to get home without missing the key moment in the Yankee-Seattle game I was watching in one of the writer's offices while we waited for the editor to work his will on the stories about urban blacks, American families, Reagan's rise, Cuban riots and the prison escape of former horse trainer Buddy Jacobson. For five innings neither team scored, a feat the Mariners accomplished easily. Then in the sixth, technical difficulties knocked out the picture from Seattle and Bobby Murcer hit an upper-deck shot (we were told) that turned out to be the only run the Yankees needed. I went back to my office and put on my radio. While I had been waiting for the elevator, Bobby Brown had hit a two-run homer.

It turned out that I didn't miss anything during a cab ride home—both because no more runs were scored and because the cabdriver had a TV set on in the front seat! It has never happened before and may never happen again, and I am not sure I like the idea of a cabbie watching TV as he drives up Broadway. But I made it home safely in time to see John finish a two-hit shutout for his 200th career victory. In one place or another I had watched maybe six of the game's nine innings, and in terms of action the best I saw was Tommy John leaning into the stands to kiss his wife when the game was over.

Saturday, June 7. I *saw* the key play in tonight's game—and saw it on the replay, too. The problem this time was that the home-plate and third-base umpires didn't see it. Batting with two strikes on him in the second inning, Reggie Jackson took one of those half swings. Did he go around far enough for a strike-out? The catcher thought so. From the broadcast booth Bill White thought so. The 48,000 fans in the Kingdome thought so, too. And after the replay shown on TV, I was sure of it.

Of course, we are currently without a national consensus as to where the line is between a checked swing and a strike. Growing up, we parroted the rule that if you break your wrists it's a strike. But TV replays have shown so many batters breaking their wrists and still having balls called that announcers now speak vaguely of "going around far enough." The *New York Times*'s Question Box addressed the issue last month and confused it further: "According to Barney Deary, head of the umpire development program for the major leagues, there is no such thing as 'breaking the wrists' and batters have smashed home runs without doing so."

But if we arrive at an understanding of what constitutes a checked swing, why not let the umpires use the instant replay to confirm or correct their decision? The arguments against any use of the replay are familiar. First, the television picture can be deceiving. This is especially true of a tag play, where a camera angle can make it look like a tag is being made by a glove that is actually several inches away from the sliding runner. Other times the camera arrives at the scene of action just after the ball. Another problem is that for many plays what happens next depends on an instantaneous call. Where do you put the runners who went back to their bases when the umpire said the outfielder caught a ball that the subsequent replay showed he really trapped? And once you introduce machines into the game, where do you stop? An electronically monitored strike zone would eliminate inconsistency between the strike zones of different umpires, not to mention thousands of ugly player glares per year. It would also bring baseball right into 1984.

All of these counterarguments are at their weakest, however, in the checked-swing situation. The swing is isolated, it takes place in clear view and in the same place every time, the call does not affect play elsewhere on the field, and it already involves an appeal to a second umpire. A monitor could be set up at the end of each dugout, where the managers and the umpires could watch the replay when an appeal is made. And the fans could watch on the scoreboard replay and vote with their applause, like on a TV game show.

Do I favor such a step? Only if I turn my back on a century of tradition and am willing to accept a breach in the basic humanity of the game. An umpire's right to make a bad call is probably not in the Constitution alongside every citizen's right to express a misguided opinion, but they both make life a lot more interesting.

But an appeal to the replay machine sure would have helped tonight. If the umps had viewed the replay of Reggie's swing, they would have called him out. They didn't, he wasn't, and three pitches later he hit a home run that won the game for the Yankees, 1–0.

Monday, June 9. Don't tell *me*, Howard, that TV doesn't call the shots, when I see that ABC's Monday Night Baseball game is starting in Anaheim at 5:30 P.M. ABC got the idea for this game in years past when California had Nolan Ryan. Putting

Nolan Ryan on at dusk is the closest anyone has yet come to scheduling a no-hitter on East Coast prime-time TV. Of course, California no longer has Nolan Ryan—or any pitching at all. But even more important for the ratings, California is playing the Yankees. The first four nationally scheduled Monday night games of this television year have all involved the Yankees or the Dodgers. Network TV's cardinal rule is play it safe.

A 5:30 start is fine for everybody except the fans who have to get to the game and the players who have to hit pitches flying through the twilight. But how many players and live fans are there compared to the millions of zombies out here in TV-land? Howard, who made his reputation by telling it like it is, will not, however, complain that TV's presence is interfering with the sport, any more than he complained last fall when the big bucks of TV produced a World Series largely played in the numbing cold of October nights plus a Sunday game scheduled late in the afternoon so as not to interfere with pro football. On the contrary, Howard kept attacking the idiots who blamed ABC for the terrible weather. TV was not "responsible," he repeatedly said, using a logic that he must have picked up in law school.

Howard widened the credibility gap, and confirmed the generally accepted view that he knows very little about the game (as opposed to the history) of baseball, by continually proclaiming that we were watching a "great" Series. The weather was terrible, the Baltimore defense was atrocious, the Pirate infielders made jokes about their own fielding, the Oriole pitching was a disappointment and the Pittsburgh staff was a patchwork of ancients.

The Series had no story or hero (including Omar Moreno's whistle-blowing wife) until the seventh game when Willie Stargell hit a game-winning home run. Until that point, ironically, Howard had been describing Stargell as one of the Series' goats.

Enough. I have faulted TV for playing it safe, and what could be safer than attacking Howard Cosell?

Tuesday, June 10. Last night's game with California was sickening. It wasn't helped by the nasal voice of play-by-play announcer Al Michaels or the intrusive, obstreperous, obnoxious and pompous presence of Howard Cosell, but I will withhold my complaints about baseball on ABC. Last night was something worse: a game that got away.

Much to the apparent surprise of the California bench, they were ahead 4–0 with but three innings to play. A solo homer by Joe Lefebvre ended the Yankees' string of scoreless innings at twenty-two. Then Freddie Patek got nobody on a doubleplay ball, and two-out doubles by Spencer and Jackson tied the game. When the Yankees added two in the eighth, the Angels appeared to have lost again. But California miraculously rallied for three runs on only one solid hit—a clutch double by Rod Carew—for a 7–6 lead going into the ninth.

The Yankees didn't need to win this game but California, with the majors' second-worst record, did. Unfortunately, the Angels have no relief pitching and the Yankees do. I said to California manager Jim Fregosi, "Is this the best we have?" as rag-armed Dave LaRoche, his Cleveland fastball just a memory, took the mound in the ninth. One swing by Reggie tied the game and—5:30 start notwithstanding—I went to bed rather than face the dubious prospect of extra innings. It turned out that it took the Yankees only one more inning to return the Angels to their misery.

Wednesday, June 11. With five major league teams located in the state of California, why are the Angels the ones that get to call themselves "California"? Whatever the cause, they certainly fit the California stereotype: big stars with lots of money who are from somewhere else. Look at the starting lineup they threw at the Yankees. Instead of a civic identity, it's a freeway franchise of rootless veterans, a Hollywood lot of big names randomly assembled for the latest disaster movie, *Ballpark '80!* The infield is Jason Thompson (first time in the cast after four years with Detroit!), Bobby Grich (the Oriole star!), Freddie Patek (who'll ever forget his Yankee-hating performances with the Royals?) and the Angels' own Carney Lansford. In the outfield are Joe Rudi (a winner for Oakland!), Rick Miller (seven seasons a Red Sock) and Larry Harlow (off a bit part with the Birds). And don't forget the DH, Rod Carew (you loved him in Minnesota!). It is hardly worth mentioning pitching in a disaster like this one, but tonight we saw the Angels' newest free-agent hope for the '80s, Bruce Kison (coming off a nine-year run in Pittsburgh). If well-known names guaranteed a winner, this team wouldn't be in last place. Then again, no one ever said *Airport '79* was a good movie.

Thursday, June 12. "The boat is not as calm as it seems," were the ominous words from bench sitter Bobby Murcer after the Yankees' surprise 5–4 loss to the Angels Tuesday night. And Willie Randolph commented on TV the night before that Reggie was bound to do something sooner or later that would get between him and the other guys. But Willie said that wouldn't affect the way the boat played on the field, and Murcer supported that with his bat when he pinch-hit two runs home in the eleventh last night for a 9–7 Yankee win. Do these tremors indicate an explosion to come, or are these just routine shiftings along the Yankee fault lines? The only thing we can be sure of is that the *Post*'s Mike Marley and his confreres will be only too happy to let us know when the boat starts rocking.

Murcer's outburst led to another case study, this one of the "every complaint brings a reaction" variety, from chief boatrocker George Steinbrenner. "Ballplayers should do their talking with their bats and gloves and not with their mouths," said Steinbrenner. Steinbrenner apparently does not recognize any comparable rule for owners, such as "Owners should do their talking with their wallets and not with their mouths." The day before, watching the game on TV in Florida, Steinbrenner disagreed with an umpire's calls and telephoned the press box to dictate a press release: "I am tired of bad calls by umpire Fred Spenn, who last year was one of the umpires who broke the strike. I still don't feel he's a capable major league umpire." Come to think of it, if the league office still has any rules about publicly disparaging umpires, and if it has the guts to enforce them, Steinbrenner may get the chance to express himself with his wallet after all.

Friday, June 13. While the Yankees had an off-day in California, New York's other team completed an improbable three-game sweep of the Dodgers at Shea. The most visible change wrought by the Mets' new owners this year was to hire an ad agency that created the preposterous slogan "The Magic Is Back." The Mets, in fact, had changed less over the winter than almost any team in the league—and last year they finished in last place, easily. So how was the magic back?

After much well-deserved abuse and a somewhat silly fine by the Commissioner—not for the misleading ads but for a rather more truthful comment that the South Bronx was not the safest place in the world to visit—the beleaguered ad-agency president admitted that the slogan should have been slanted slightly more toward the future, like "The magic is coming back." Even that seemed overly optimistic during the first six weeks of the season. But suddenly the Mets started to turn one-run losses into one-run wins, and a rookie reliever named Neil Allen began acting like the Tug McGraw of 1973. If they can continue playing like they have in the last seven days, when they have come from behind to take six of seven games from Pittsburgh and L.A., we may see proof once again of the time-worn cliché, the truth is stranger than ad copy.

I am not a particular Mets fan—the kind of person who

can name all the original Mets or their sixty-six third basemen
—and I doubt that any serious Yankee-hater is. The Yankee-
hater tends to be a serious baseball student—and that means a
student of serious baseball. The Mets have been amusing, entertaining and occasionally miraculous, but the average level
of play over their eighteen-year existence has left much to be
desired. In an effort to create an instant following, management sacrificed serious baseball values to crowd pleasing,
bringing back such New York favorites as Casey Stengel, Gil
Hodges, Yogi Berra, Duke Snider and Willie Mays, no matter how far over the hill it found them. The Long Island location of the new Shea Stadium, more convenient to suburban
autos than inner-city public transportation, helped establish
a new clientele, a crowd different from the ones that had grown
up in Ebbets Field or the Polo Grounds. And finally, there
was the stadium itself—a round, characterless symmetrical
cliché—typical of the modern, all-purpose stadium that serves
equally well, or poorly, for baseball, football and rock con-
certs. In contrast to Yankee Stadium, Shea had no bleachers
and had an exposed upper deck that was so far from the field
that it was hard not to lose interest in the game and watch, instead, the airplanes that flew overhead every 135 seconds.

The Yankees had tradition, the Mets were today. Before
the Steinbrenner era, going to home games of the two teams
was something like shopping in Tiffany's versus Blooming-
dale's. At Shea, you couldn't hear yourself think. Aside from
the 707s buzzing the stadium, there was always a crowd of
30,000, at least half of whom were preteenagers who never
got tired of yelling and hadn't learned that others might get
tired of listening to them. Most of them came in groups, like
the Little League team from Bethpage. When they weren't
screaming "Let's go Mets," or cheering the appearance of
their names on the inane message board, they were carrying
around banners, another trademark of the Mets fan. For those
who couldn't make it to the game, there was the absolutely
colorless radio and TV-broadcast team which has yet to criti-

cize an umpire, second-guess a manager, or suggest that a player was putting out less than a 100 percent effort. In short, the Mets hardly provided a satisfying atmosphere for the experienced baseball scholar.

Meanwhile over at Yankee Stadium, you found the old-timers who had watched Mantle and DiMaggio, if not Ruth and Gehrig, and had a sense of history; who appreciated the quiet beauty of the game, and didn't need an organist's piping to fill in every lull in the action; who knew the umpires' names and appreciated that a manager's job was something more than merely to revive memories of five years ago. Of course, Steinbrenner is changing all this now, but these were the differences, and how real they were, in the Mets' first decade, when people in and around New York began to be classified as Yankee fans or Mets fans.

That said, the fact remains that the Mets, as the second team in town, were in competition with the Yankees. I could not like the Mets on their own merits, perhaps, but to the extent that they could give the Yankees a hard time, I found myself rooting for them. Fortunately for New York, the Mets' period of glory, 1969–73, coincided with the Yankees' deepest depression. I could watch the Yankees grovel—that team of Horace Clarke, Bobby Murcer and Roy White—and I didn't have to worry about the overall psychic health of my city. Since the Yankees have come back, the Mets have floundered, and I have at least the same sympathy for them as I do for underdogs everywhere, including those in Atlanta.

Saturday, June 14. Those Mets took me back twenty years tonight. I had turned on the radio merely for background noise as I did the dishes, especially when I heard that the score was 6–2 in favor of the San Francisco Giants in the ninth. I wasn't thinking of another miracle comeback, and neither was the announcer, who was already into his wrap-up and speaking with corporate optimism of the chances for a Met win *tomorrow*. Two infield outs sandwiching a bunt single brought the Giants within one easy out of their second straight win. A walk prolonged the matter, Mazzilli gave the fans solace with an RBI single, and Claudell Washington gave hope for the future with his first National League hit. Hey wait a minute, that made the score 6–4 and brought the winning run to the plate, in the person of Steve Henderson, the National League's leading hitter. No matter that Henderson had not hit a home run all year, he hit one now to cap a two-out five-run rally and give the Mets a 7–6 win.

Twenty years ago I listened to the Pittsburgh Pirates do the same thing, night in and night out, over WWVA from Wheeling, West Virginia. My family lived in the suburbs of New York, but my father and his ancestors were from Pittsburgh. I grew up with stories of days spent at Forbes Field watching the great teams of Pie Traynor, Paul and Lloyd Waner and Arky Vaughan. The nicknamed baseball legend I adopted for my own was the Flying Dutchman, not the Bambino or the Georgia Peach, and we spoke of Ralph Kiner in terms of awe that other boys were taught to use for DiMaggio or Williams. But the Pittsburgh Pirate teams of my youth were so bad—from 1950 through 1957 they finished last six times and seventh twice—that it wasn't until I was fourteen years old that I wholeheartedly acknowledged my "roots." The Pirates of 1960 would go into the ninth with a no-hitter being thrown at them and come out on top. Radio announcer Bob Prince shamelessly led the cheering, urging Groat and Stuart to hit a "bloop and a blast" to send us home. The players all had, or were given by Prince, distinct and engaging personalities: Vern "Deacon" Law was backed up by "the Baron of the Bullpen," ElRoy Face. Forrest "Smoky" Burgess did the catching, and the outfield was Bob "Dog" Skinner, Bill "Quail" Virdon and Roberto "Arriba" Clemente. "Tiger" Hoak played third, and "Ducky" Schofield was the infield reserve. They were a team of destiny and they knew it.

The rest of the world knew it, too, after they beat the Yankees in one of the most memorable World Series of all times. I had, perhaps not coincidentally, been an avid Dodger fan when Brooklyn beat the Yankees in 1955. By 1957, with the Dodgers headed for the West Coast, I had shifted allegiance to the Milwaukee Braves, and I gloried in the Braves' triumph that year over the Yankees. But both of those immensely satisfying wins fell short of providing the personal vindication I received in 1960. No one else I knew claimed to be a Pirate fan, and when asked my reason I could proudly cite family tradition and talk about a radio station that none of my friends had even heard of. By World Series time I had quite an investment in the Pirates.

Moreover, their World Series opponent was a New York Yankee team that, even to an objective mind, had little appeal. Just when it had looked like the American League might be opening up, thanks to the Yankees' third-place finish in 1959, the 1960 team had come back as strong as ever to win by eight games, Casey Stengel's tenth pennant in twelve years as Yankee manager. The team was comprised in equal parts of detested leftovers from the early '50s—Berra, Mantle, McDougald, Skowron, Ford—colorless but efficient drones who had come of age in the Eisenhower years—Richardson, Kubek, Howard, Blanchard, Coates—and a horde of imports from Kansas City—Ditmar, Terry, Shantz, Lopez, Cerv and Maris. The gutsy, opportunistic Pirates, representing a city which last won the World Championship in 1925, were matched against the methodical, characterless Yankees, who had won six world championships in the last decade.

Baseball has seen nothing like the first six games of that World Series. The Yankees absolutely routed the Pirates three times, 16–3, 10–0 and 12–0, while the Pirates won three low-scoring games, 6–4, 3–2 and 5–2. That set the stage for perhaps the greatest Game 7 in World Series history. In those days the World Series was played in the afternoon, when I had to go to school, but it was fitting that I listened to the culminating moments of this season on my radio—even if it meant carrying it out to soccer practice. I was putting my books in my locker when Hal "Hawk" Smith hit his dramatic three-run homer in the eighth to transform a sure loss into an equally sure victory. My next memory is Mickey Mantle slipping back to first under Rocky Nelson's tag, thwarting a game-ending doubleplay and helping the Yankees tie the game in the ninth at 9–9. And then, with the noise of jumping jacks in the background—"Who do we beat/Who do we beat/Oss-ning/Oss-ning"—I heard one of the great moments in Pittsburgh and Yankee-hater history: Bill Mazeroski's ninth-inning leadoff home run over the leftfield wall, the perfect ending to a once-in-a-lifetime season.

The 1960 Pirates had a better pedigree than the 1980 Mets, having finished second and fourth the two previous years, and they weren't still striving to reach .500 on June 15, so I won't push the analogy too far at this time. But just in case there is a miracle and we have our first 60-cent Subway Series, I want it known that I was with the Mets all the way.

Sunday, June 15. Chapter 1 of Billy Martin Squares Off Against the Yankees was a bomb, a bust, a fizz. Not only did the Yankees win three of four games from Oakland, they won them in the most dispiriting fashion: a seventh-inning grand slam by Reggie on Friday night for a 6–4 win; a two-out, two-strike, two-run ninth-inning homer by Murcer on Saturday for a 2–1 win; and a four-hitter by Tiant with two home runs by Reggie on Sunday for an 8–2 laugher. The three crowds totaled 121,364, which was an all-time Oakland record, but most of those people were wearing Yankee caps and carrying signs that said Massapequa, N.Y. Loves the Yankees.

We didn't even get to see any of the daring baserunning and unorthodox strategy that Martin has installed to differentiate his club from the Seattle Mariners. Part of this was more the fault of WPIX than Martin, for they had decided back in January not to televise Friday night's doubleheader. At that time, of course, Martin had not been hired by Oakland,

and the prospect of a doubleheader with the worst team in the majors carrying on until 3:30 in the morning probably made dead air sound exciting in comparison.

But that first game turned out to be the highlight of the series. Martin tried beanballs and stealing home, neither of which worked, but he got a ninth-inning home run from another mistreated former Yankee, Mickey Klutts, for a 4–3 win over Guidry. Oakland led 4–2 after six innings of the second game, too. Then Reggie managed, once again, to get the better of Billy Martin. His grand slam not only won that game, it decided the next two as well.

I watched on Saturday as Oakland pitcher Rick Langford and Figueroa matched three-hitters for eight innings in the dull kind of afternoon game to be expected after a late-night doubleheader. I would be entertained enough, however, if I could see the Yankees lose, which was possible on the strength of the run Oakland scored in the first. But when Reggie interrupted his time at bat in the seventh to pick up a hot dog wrapper that was two-thirds of the way to first base, I could sense his ego starting to crush Oakland's confidence. Reggie only hit a single in the ninth, to Langford's palpable relief, but it was enough to give the suddenly controversial Murcer a chance to bat. The count went to 0–2. Martin goes crazy if his pitcher loses a game on an 0–2 pitch, so instructions to waste a pitch were hand-carried to the mound. How much better Billy felt about losing it on a 1–2 pitch I don't know, but that is what happened when Murcer barely lifted a hanging slider over the rightfield fence.

Reggie didn't wait so long today. His tape-measure job to center in the first inning buried the A's in a hole from which they never emerged. As for Billy's baserunners, in two days I didn't see an attempted steal of second, let alone a double steal or a suicide squeeze. Then again, as the baseball axiom—or is it a Chinese proverb?—has it, you can't steal home if you don't get to first.

Tuesday, June 17. The Yankees swept through the West Coast like pillagers last week, the battered victims are now limping back through Yankee Stadium, and it is pathetic. When they are not playing the Yankees, the A's, Angels and Mariners are being beat up on by the Red Sox and Orioles. I hate to say I told you so, but the Yankees have opened up a 6½-game lead in their division before they have to face Boston and Cleveland for the first time all year.

Howser had an everybody-gets-to-play game tonight, an 8–2 laugher over Seattle and its supposed ace, Rick Honeycutt. It's a good thing, too, for the troops are getting restless once again. This time it is Piniella who is outspoken about his lack of playing time, which means the Yankees can now platoon Murcer and Piniella as designated griper on the bench. What makes the situation more than a laughing matter is that not only do the Yankees currently have five outfielders who want to play every day, two more—Ruppert Jones and Oscar Gamble —are expected back off the disabled list in the next two weeks. Howser knows this is coming, so he has been giving everybody —even Dennis Werth got to DH last night—lots of chances in the games against second-rate opposition, hoping, I suspect, that a few slumps and a few hot streaks will eliminate some of the hard decisions.

The biggest problem for Piniella and Murcer is Joe Lefebvre, who was brought up from the minors only a month ago and has been in the lineup almost every day since. From what I've seen, Lefebvre is the best outfield prospect the Yankees have, and I am predicting he will be their rightfielder for many years to come. But for the moment his average has dropped to .260. Meanwhile Bobby Brown, who has played every day during Jones's absence, has seen his average fall from .330 to .258. This makes it a lot easier for Howser to say, "These guys have shown their potential and we'll give them every shot at beating out the old-timers next year, but for the stretch run this year I'm going to stick with the veterans who have done it before." Since Roy White is gone, that means Piniella, Murcer and Gamble.

But if Lefebvre, Brown or Werth could only play short-stop! Bucky Dent went on the disabled list Sunday with a spiked wrist, which gave a chance to one of my favorites, Chicken Stanley, a lifetime .220 hitter who incessantly complains about called strikes when he bats. But after only two days of squawking, Chicken pulled a hamstring, and the Yankees are now relying on minor league second baseman Brian Doyle. "I'm going to concede," said Steinbrenner woefully, enjoying the Yankees' biggest lead of the year.

Saturday, June 21. There was drama during the player introductions at today's Old-Timers' Day, but it was nothing like the drama of 1978, when George Steinbrenner stunned rational people all over the world by announcing that he had rehired Billy Martin to manage the Yankees for the 1980 season. This year we knew Billy would be there, because the Oakland team he wound up managing in 1980 was to play the current Yankees in the day's main event. The drama, such as it was, was whether Billy would be introduced wearing his old Yankee number 1 uniform, or, out of spite, would come on in the gold and green of the A's? He had actually played 73 games for the A's back in 1957 as he started a post-Copacabana, end-of-career trek that also carried him to Detroit, Cleveland, Cincinnati, Milwaukee, and Minnesota. But that bit of trivia wouldn't prompt Billy to appear at Old-Timers' Day in an Oakland uniform. Nor would the more logical motive of showing his new team, and the few Oakland fans that might exist, that he was proud to be an A, and wanted to be thought of as such. No, the motivating factors here were Billy's emotional ties with the Yankees and his emotional wars with their current principal owner.

Steinbrenner, the man with 52,000 tickets sold and a team comfortably in first place, was able to take a lighthearted view of the man he had fired twice: "If he won't wear the Yankee uniform, I'll pour Pepto-Bismol all over him," he said referring to a commercial the two were to tape the day before the game. Martin's comment was a touch more heavy-handed: "If George thinks I belong in that uniform, why did he fire me?" Counting the four umpires as one, which is how they were introduced, Billy's was the fifty-seventh introduction, and he came out in pinstripes.

In my youth I thought Old-Timers' Day an interminable bore, but as I grow older, I have come to appreciate it in much the same way that I now look forward to dressing up on Thanksgiving and driving to Connecticut for dinner with my father's aunts. The best part is that no matter how young the crowd becomes, the place of honor is still held for "the greatest living ballplayer," Joe DiMaggio, who has a stunning head of white hair and a great smile and, unlike Ronald Reagan, looks the way a 65-year-old legend should look. Actually, the competition for that designation at this particular game was not that impressive. After Hall-of-Famers Mantle, Berra and Ford and such second-liners as Maris, Bauer, Richardson, Henrich and Keller, the roster of Yankee returnees fell off to such trivia items as Jack Reed (129 career at-bats), Marius Russo (45 lifetime wins), and Bud Metheny. I do remember Joe Collins, but the best the TV graphic could do for him was "5th in walks on the Yankees in '52 and '53."

The team of Opponents was an extraordinarily unimpressive hodgepodge, led by former Giant-Oriole-Senator Johnny Orsino, who had trouble getting into a game in his prime. But he got two hits today, and Larry Doby and Jackie Jensen, the two most legitimate all-stars, drove balls to the outfield fence, as the Opponents built a 9–0 lead against the ex-Yankees and held on for a 9–5 win. The Yankee Hall-of-Famers, not to mention Billy Martin, didn't play in the two-inning "game," but I will take any victory over any Yankees that I can get. A rout of the old-timers is good for the soul.

Sunday, June 22. The good news is that the 17-game stretch against the hapless West Coast teams is finally over. The bad news is that the Yankees face the same three teams again for 19 straight games starting August 19. The worse news is that just when the Yankees are facing 6 games in the next ten days against the archrival Red Sox, Boston slugger Jim Rice has been put on the disabled list after a pitch chipped a bone in his wrist.

Billy Martin produced no fireworks for Oakland this weekend, either, and although the A's won two of their seven games with the Yanks, that was more a triumph for the law of averages. And if you're the one with the .714, you can't complain about averages.

Chapter 5
THE INDIANS WAX AND THE RED SOX WANE
And the Yankees Bomb Them Both

Monday, June 23. "Wanna go to the Red Sox game tonight?" one of my Boston friends asked me on the phone this afternoon. After first ascertaining that he was not offering an extra ticket in the owner's box or some equally select and protected area, I quickly and righteously declined. If Old-Timers' Day yesterday brought out the best in Yankee fans, the appearance of the Red Sox in Yankee Stadium tonight is sure to bring out the worst. The two teams may or may not hate each other now that Thurman Munson can no longer resent All-Star votes for Carlton Fisk and now that Bill Lee has taken the shoulder that Graig Nettles separated and his diatribes about "Nazis" Steinbrenner and Martin to the National League. But even if Mike Torrez came out and embraced Reggie Jackson in centerfield, where Jackson does his limbering up exercises before each game, the vendors selling Boston Sucks T-shirts would be assured of their brisk sales, for the battle in the stands has a life of its own.

When the Yankees visit Fenway Park, thousands of students from New York who are attending colleges in and around Boston go out to Fenway Park and cheer the Yankees like liberators arriving in Paris. They also thumb their noses and collect their bets from the fanatical Red Sox fans they find themselves living among for eight months of the year. And when the Sox come to New York, they prompt a pilgrimage to Yankee Stadium of every young working male who grew up in Massachusetts and who has come to the Big Apple to pursue a career. With the exception of a perverse minority of Yankee fans, everyone in New England is a Red Sox fan, and anybody leaving New England has to go through New York.

The crowds at Yankee–Red Sox games are not your Family Night, your Ladies' Day or your Senior Citizens crowds. They are not even the innocently destructive under-fourteens that fill up the Stadium for Bat Day, Helmet Day or Jockstrap Weekend. These are fans who want to see the other team lose. They are crowds of men who are young, who are out to impress the world and who drink a lot of beer. Add to this the normal collection of rowdies who like to be where the action is, who like the atmosphere of yelling, screaming and chanting obscenities, cap stealing, banner ripping and beer throwing, and you have a good idea of why I prefer to stay home and watch the Yankee–Red Sox games on TV.

Oh, one more thing: tonight's game has been delayed a half hour to accommodate the folks from ABC, who decided over the weekend that we would rather watch this game than the boring Dodgers against the Astros (who were pitching Joaquin Andujar, not Ryan or Richard). This should give the yahoos an extra half hour of lubrication before the game even begins. Last fall I attended the first Monday Night Football game ABC televised from Shea Stadium. Starting at nine o'clock, the Jets and Vikings played a game that would have put me to sleep except that fights kept breaking out in the stands—even though everyone was rooting for the same team. The game ended with a guy bouncing on the baseball backstop and people in the upper stands throwing beer down on him.

New York has been well in the forefront of a fifteen-year trend toward unruly sports crowds. And I'm not talking violent sports, like hockey, boxing and roller derby. I am referring to such formerly genteel sports as tennis and golf. Forest Hills used to attract moderate crowds of suburban tennis players, who would rarely whistle when a close call by a linesman went against their favorite player. Then, with no little help from such bad actors as Ilie Nastase and Jimmy Connors and the increasing commercialization of the sport, the scene changed. On my last visit to Forest Hills, 10,000 fans stood and chanted, "We won't go," when management canceled a scheduled match so as not to interfere with a separate-admission evening program. Last year, with the Open shifted to Flushing Meadows, across the subway tracks from Shea Stadium, a crowd riot not only forced the umpire to change a call, it also forced the tournament director to change the umpire.

New Yorkers were able to show off their golf etiquette last week when the U.S. Open was played at northern New Jersey's Baltusrol Club. Television viewers could watch Jack Nicklaus sink a fifteen-foot birdie putt to win the event—and almost get trampled as a result. One section of the crowd swarmed like the Italian army across a sand trap even as Nicklaus lined up his putt.

Some sports commentators tried to turn this rowdiness into a spontaneous outpouring of affection for the veteran Nicklaus. There was some of that talk, too, when the Shea Stadium infield was torn up after the Mets won the pennant in 1973. But it was pretty hard not to recognize wanton destruction and disrespect of other human beings as the sheer ugliness it is when this strain of behavior reached a peak of sorts in the 1976 Playoffs at Yankee Stadium. That was the year that Steinbrenner brought the Yankees their first pennant in 12 years. They did it in the fifth game of the Playoffs against Kansas City, when Chris Chambliss led off the bottom of the tenth with a home run. Onto the field poured a swarming mass of fans—seemingly all 20-year-old males bent on acquiring souvenirs from Yankee players, including Chambliss who was still rounding the bases. Halfway to third he realized his predicament, and he started knocking people down. He came home like a fullback trying to get through the Atlanta Falcons and we will never know whether he ever touched home plate (one story was that he went back out an hour after the game just to make sure). What should have been the greatest moment of his sporting life, a majestic sweep around the bases with the pennant-winning run, became instead a moment of terror.

Since then at Yankee Stadium, the players know that when a big game is over, you grab your glove, your hat and your glasses and run to the dugout and save the congratulations for the locker room. The "spontaneous exuberance" of the fans is usually plotted well in advance and is fortified by three hours of beer drinking. It is no more a part of the game than having your tires slashed while your car is in the Stadium parking lot. My solution would be to station machine gun—carrying special forces on the foul lines after the game with instructions to open fire at knee level the moment anyone stepped on the field. Leftover liberals might not like it, but I suspect that it would do the trick.

Monday, June 23. Tonight, I hope, was the first day of the rest of the season, as the Red Sox brought the Yankees a bit closer to earth, not to mention Milwaukee, with a 7–2 trouncing. The Yankees' second loss in a row was filled with delicious moments. For starters, Eckersley beat Guidry. Yastrzemski hit a majestic two-run homer to right. Bobby Brown misplayed two balls in center field. Randolph threw high and wide to the plate, allowing one run to score and setting up another. Tony Perez, the Red Sox' replacement for Bob Watson, drove in two runs to increase his league-leading total to 53. Reggie was stifled, hitting two easy grounders and a broken-bat single. The only Yankee runs were solo shots in the first and eighth by Joe Lefebvre: after the first Eckersley tossed the resin bag and smiled, after the second he just shrugged. The Yankees can't use the absence of Dent, Jones and Murcer as an excuse, either, for Boston was playing without Rice, Fisk and Remy and with a hamstrung Hobson limited to DH'ing. Before last night I had never even *heard* of two players in the Boston starting lineup—Stapleton and Hoffman.

Even though, or maybe because, the Yankees were losing badly, the fans behaved about as I expected, prompting Howard Cosell to give a little lecture on "rowdyism" and prompting Boston rightfielder Dwight Evans to don a batting helmet to ward off unfriendly missiles in right field, including a lead sinker.

Reggie was not completely shut out of the national spotlight. After he walked in the *first* inning, he pulled some candy in an orange wrapper out of his pocket and had a snack while standing on first base. Please don't tell me it was a Reggie bar!

Tuesday, June 24. "Boston's rivalry with New York is total," my Irish friend from Melrose, Massachusetts, explained to me as we watched the Red Sox play the Yankees on TV. "Ever since New York passed Boston as the dominant port city on the East Coast, Boston has felt itself in competition with New York. But while New York grew huge and adopted a worldly-wise, money-can-buy-anything attitude, Boston remained a backwater. It was parochial in its world view. But the people in Boston always felt that while New York was bigger, Boston was better. Unlike New York, Boston had class.

"The Boston sports fan is a purist, too. He takes his sports very seriously. And the team managements find players who relate to the city. Look at the guys who are stars in Boston—Carlton Fisk, Dave Cowens, John Havlicek. They are dedicated athletes who give everything to their sport and are part of the community. They appear at Jimmy Fund fundraisers and speak at Little League dinners. Compare this with

New York. The stars here are guys like Joe Namath, Walt Frazier and of course Reggie, guys who drive Cadillacs and Rolls-Royces and hang out in East Side bars.

"Every kid in the Boston area is a Red Sox fan. You start when you play in Little League and your team goes to Fenway Park and you sit together out in the rightfield stands. Then you go to college in Boston and you sit with all the college kids in the bleachers. Look at the two ballparks. At Fenway you're right on the field, you can see the players, it's a personal, friendly, family atmosphere. Yankee Stadium is like New York: it's big, impersonal and cold.

"The attitude toward the Yankees used to be tinged with awe, back in the '50s and early '60s when the Yankees were so good. Ever since the Sox won in '67, however, Boston thought it could beat the Yankees, and there has been a lot of frustration when the Red Sox lost. I don't have to tell you about the last couple of years."

And why do Yankee fans, with their established dominance and cosmopolitan world view, care so much about beating Boston? First is the presence of so many Red Sox fans in New York. Everyone knows at least one fanatical Red Sox fan who will lord it over him if Boston beats the Yankees. And there are always enough Red Sox fans at the Stadium to goad the macho Yankee supporters into louder obscenities and ruder behavior. Second is the fact that the Red Sox have had a genuinely competitive team on the field. While Baltimore may have had a better record than Boston over the last fifteen years, the Orioles have not had the superstars—like Yaz, Rice, Lynn and Fisk—that Yankee fans could recognize as individual rivals for their own heroes.

And so tonight there were again more than 40,000 fans at Yankee Stadium screaming and chanting as the Yanks turned the tables with a 10–5 win that included a game-turning pop-fly home run by Cerone and a predictable three-run coup de grace by Reggie. And oh yes, there was also a smoke bomb thrown onto the field and wildly jubilant fans who ran out during the game to meet Reggie and try to borrow Gossage's cap while he was pitching.

Thursday, June 26. A good working definition of the word "ambivalence" is what I feel when Commissioner Bowie Kuhn issues a ruling against the Yankees. Today's case in point involves Billy Cannon, Jr., an 18-year-old shortstop from Baton Rouge, Louisiana, who is the son of the best college football player of 1959. His father garnered more notoriety—and this is important background to the current controversy—by becoming the first top collegian to sign with the fledgling American Football League. He signed his contract with the Houston Oilers in front of 80,000 fans after the Sugar Bowl Game— and became the object of a court fight when it turned out that he had already signed a contract with the Los Angeles Rams, too.

The competitive leagues that proliferated during the sports boom of the '60s have now all died or been absorbed, and the monopolistic trend of big-league sports is returning with a vengeance. Baseball even took a page from football's book in 1965 and instituted an amateur draft to avoid competitive bidding situations and the higher bonuses and salaries that would result. Billy Cannon, Sr., realized that how much young Billy would be offered depended on whether he was drafted by a cheapskate like Minnesota's Calvin Griffith or by a big spender like New York's George Steinbrenner. Unable to play one team or one league off against another, Dr. Cannon, now an orthodontist, had only one bargaining chip: if young Billy wasn't offered enough money, he would—what a threat!—go to college. When it appeared that most teams were not willing to guarantee Billy $100,000 when he turned 21, Dr. Cannon sent telegrams to all teams advising them not to waste a draft pick. This convinced everybody except the Yankees, who proceeded to draft Billy with the first pick they had. Four American League rivals, including the always suspicious Blue Jays, smelled foul play—or was it just Stein-

brenner's normal odor?—and asked the Commissioner to investigate the possibility that Cannon's telegrams were a ruse
designed to thwart the draft system. Kuhn's ruling, based on
"inferences," not only voided the Yankees' pick, it barred
them from drafting young Billy in the future. Although the
result is welcome, I have a hard time accepting the procedures
employed in reaching it. There is an unpleasantly dictatorial
quality about Kuhn's acting, as he frequently does, as prose-
cuting attorney, judge and jury—not to mention court of
highest appeal. Even in the company of a devious father and
an unscrupulous owner, the conclusion remains that this Baseball Commissioner is the loosest cannon of them all.

Friday, June 27. The practically all-new Cleveland Indians
came to town tonight, but the pitcher and manager were hold-
overs and they reenacted, wtih one key difference, the final
scene of the last game I saw the Indians play in 1979. Lefthander Rick Waits, despite a 5.60 ERA, was pitching a 2–0
shutout going into the ninth. With one out, Bob Watson singled up the middle, Eric Soderholm lined a hit to left and
Cleveland manager Dave Garcia came out of the dugout.
Two years ago Waits beat Catfish Hunter on the final day
of the season, which was the last game the Tribe had won in
New York. With one on in the ninth last October, Garcia lifted
Waits and a 2–1 lead wound up a 5–2 loss. Last night Garcia
left Waits in the game and Dennis Werth hit into a game-
ending doubleplay. My heart slowly eased its way back down
my throat.

   With an infield of Soderholm, Doyle, Randolph and
Werth, an outfield of Piniella, Brown and Murcer, and Rudy
May making his first start on only two days' rest, the Yankees
looked like just another team and picked up their fourth loss
in five games. The biggest of those was in the third game with
the Red Sox. It gave Boston the series and came at the ex-
pense of Tommy John and Graig Nettles, whose tenth-inning
error set up the winning run. And Tom Burgmeier was the

best relief pitcher the Yankees have faced all year, which could psychologically neutralize the Gossage edge in the two teams' games to come.

Saturday, June 28. Who would have expected the Cleveland Indians, bouncing along at .500 with nine guys and a manager you never heard of, to attract 42,000 people to Yankee Stadium? Not me, as I dragooned my wife and two friends for a Saturday night up in the Bronx. Granted, it was "Jacket Weekend," but so was the next game, and given that choice you'd expect the horde of kids to be there on Sunday afternoon, not Saturday night. But once again I learned, never underestimate the attraction of giving something away for free. No matter that it is junk. Or that while the jacket, made of fine vinyl, does have a Yankee symbol on the left sleeve, it has McDonald's golden arches on the right sleeve—not exactly the kind of thing you'd see on Bucky and Stormy Dent. As an unadvertised bonus, we were entertained before the game by the "McDonald's All-Star Jazz Ensemble," playing and singing their rendition of that jazz classic "We Do It All for You."

On the minus side of Jacket Night, our friends were caught in traffic and we missed batting practice, lines at the concession stands were twenty minutes long all night, and the closest upper level reserve seats to home plate we could get were in section 7, which meant we couldn't see the right-field corner. On the plus side, my wife got to sit next to the cutest 9-year-old boy from Darien, Connecticut, who was attending his first baseball game and had with him all his Yankee baseball cards. The two of them traded baseball insights, such as where Reggie Jackson would be standing if he were in the game, until 10:30, when the boy's father took him back to Darien. "Who cares about a free jacket," I heard my wife thinking, "where can I get a little boy like that?"

Although someone two rows behind me couldn't believe it the first time I stood up and cheered for the Tribe, I wasn't the only Indian fan in section 7. Over to our left were five people who, I found out when the same busybody questioned *them,* were from Youngstown, Ohio. One was particularly devoted, with a cardboard sign proclaiming "Indian Fever" pinned to the front of his overalls, and an endearing habit of chanting "The Tribe is Hot, the Tribe is Hot," on his way to the men's room.

We both had plenty to cheer about during the game, but so did the 40,000 people rooting for the Yankees in what was the most action-filled game I have ever attended. Cleveland's league-leading on-base percentage of .360 went even higher as the Indians got fourteen hits, seven walks and two men on through errors. The Yankees, second in that category at .350, weren't far behind with eleven hits, seven walks and three hit batters. There were four home runs—including three of the Yankees' first four hits—and disputed calls by each of the four umpires. We even got to see the injured Reggie Jackson, who was sent up to pinch-hit on one leg in the eighth and got a walk that hitting hero Bobby Murcer (3-for-4, five RBIs, and the old Nippy Jones shoe-polish-on-ball hit-batsman trick) turned into the tying run with a two-out single just off the first baseman's glove. The only thing we didn't see was good pitching, as five Cleveland and four New York pitchers all gave up runs. The best of the bunch was Yankee lefty Tim Lollar, making his major league debut. From the upper deck, he was a mirror image of Goose Gossage, minus about twenty pounds, and he could claim the only 1-2-3 inning of the entire night.

I have put off as long as I can the painful news that Cleveland lost. They had the game well in hand, leading at various points 5–3, 8–4, and 9–6. Tough-luck pitcher Wayne Garland had made it through five innings and stood to pick up the win. Even when the Yankees came back to tie the game 9–9 in the eighth, all was not lost because Cleveland got three singles off Gossage to go ahead again, as manager Dick Howser futilely shifted Nettles and Dennis Werth back and forth between third base and shortstop. But the Yankees now had momentum and they made their task in the bottom of the ninth look easy: single by Watson, single by Spencer, sacrifice bunt by Piniella, intentional walk to Brown, and two-strike single punched to right by Cerone. If we play this badly and you still can't put us away, the Yankees said, then we will go ahead and beat you. Fortunately, we caught the "D" train right away and made our connection at 59th Street with no wait and were home twenty-five minutes after Spencer crossed the plate.

Sunday, June 29. The home run is a crude, blunt instrument. With it in your arsenal, you don't need speed, intelligence, teamwork, strategy, momentum, or even good luck. It can strike out of a blue sky and make a mockery of the subtleties and intricacies that have preceded it. It is the quickest and surest way to score runs and is far and away the least interesting. It is also a trademark of the New York Yankees.

Their nickname is the Bronx Bombers, which is apt but not very appealing. Even pro football nicknames, like the Fearsome Foursome or the Steel Curtain, do not imply so much in the area of wanton destruction. But the name fits the character of all the good Yankee teams since Babe Ruth joined the club and invented the home run in 1920. And it describes one reason for hating the champion Yankees: they don't just beat you, they bludgeon you. Other great teams had a more appealing character: there was the Gashouse Gang of St. Louis, the Whiz Kids of Philadelphia, the Go-Go Sox of Chicago, the Kiddie Korps of Baltimore, the Miracle Mets, the malcontents of Oakland, the Family of Pittsburgh. But nothing so folksy or romantic with the Yankees. They never win a pennant on spirit or divine intervention. They don't build runs with stolen bases, bunts and doubles to the opposite-field corner. Nor do they do it with great pitching: many years they have won the pennant without any 20-game winners. You never got the feeling that the Yankees were playing over their heads, that a group of mortals had meshed to produce a once-in-a-lifetime magical moment. No, the Yankees always won because somebody would hit a home run. Into the right-field seats. In the bad years the character of the team never changed, it was just that the home-run hitters—Pepitone, Murcer, an aging Mantle—weren't as good.

Now the Yankee home-run hitters are back with a vengeance. If Guidry and John are the ones who kept the Yankees competitive during the first month of the season, it is the home-run hitters who are responsible for the Yankees' rise to a commanding position in the last six weeks. Today was a typical Yankee home-run victory—and a typical frustration for singles-hitting Cleveland. The Indians got four hits off Guidry and threatened in the first and third innings but couldn't score. Cleveland pitcher Len Barker was coasting along, in no trouble, until Jim Spencer lofted a high fly into the rightfield stands for a quick 2–0 lead. Cleveland struggled back to tie the game, then in the sixth Joe Lefebvre popped one 345 feet and the score jumped to 5–2. The Indians were ahead in hits but had effectively lost the game. My point, and the coffin nail, were hammered home in the next inning when lefty-swinging Brian Doyle pulled a pitch 325 feet down the line for his first major league home run. It also happened to be the Yankees' 100th home run of the year. Cleveland has 43, the Mets have 22.

Spencer, Lefebvre and Doyle did it today. Saturday night Bobby Murcer hit two. Jackson is leading the league with 18 and former home-run champion Nettles has 13. Bobby Brown has 8 so far and don't forget Oscar Gamble, who is just off the disabled list. The righthanders have chipped in for 30 of their own, but it's the lefthanded Yankee Stadium stroke that has done the most damage and taken the fun out of so many games this season. Today's Yankee win was cold, decisive, brutal and dull. There were no rallies, no daring baserunning, no close plays at the plate, no hit-and-run or stolen bases. There were three swings of the bat for six runs and Cleveland went off to Detroit, a 7–2 loser.

Wednesday, July 2. Compared to the famous Boston Massacre of 1978, when the Yankees arrived in Fenway Park down four games and swept the series by scores of 15–3, 13–2, 7–0 and 7–4, this week's sweep of the Red Sox was less a wipeout than a wimp-out. The Red Sox were technically "in" every game. I say "technically" because although they were in position to win each night, they never looked like they expected to win. Except for the bedlam of over-sellout crowds banging on the fences, these games could well have been played in Toronto.

With Rice disabled, Fisk recuperating and Evans not hitting, Boston's fabled righthanded power just isn't there. By Wednesday night Lynn and Yastrzemski weren't playing either, which made the Red Sox worse than just another team. Which about sums up the level of opposition for the month of June. Only a four-game set over the July 4 weekend in Cleveland stands in their way before the Yankees can claim to have utterly annihilated the A's, Mariners, Angels, Red Sox and Indians in succession.

Thursday, July 3. Twenty-seven years of rooting for the Cleveland Indians paid off tonight. Before 73,096 people Wayne Garland threw a two-hitter, the Tribe hitters collected 12 singles, and the Indians stopped the Yankees' five-game winning streak cold, 7–0.

I can but poorly describe how beautiful the Indian's royal-blue home uniforms looked through the outfield camera, with the cerulean backstop behind them. And to see, and hear, a full Municipal Stadium on a perfect summer night for baseball—what a perfect vision of America for a Fourth of July weekend! The holiday—and the postgame fireworks display—was part of the lure for the major leagues' biggest crowd in seven years. An important element was the upbeat Indians' team: although they are back under .500, after losing five of six games to Detroit over the last ten days, their .278 hitting keeps them in every game. And in Joe Charboneau they have a popular rookie power hitter with the ear-marks of a homegrown star, what the Tigers are looking for in Kirk Gibson. But the extra added attraction that produced such a heavenly evening was the 1980 Cleveland debut of the New York Yankees.

After they swept the Red Sox, many people, including me, were just about ready to concede the division title to the Yankees. But that didn't mean the season, or my interest in it, was anywhere near an end. Not by a long shot. For there are still 87 games left on the regular season schedule, which means 87 opportunities for a Yankee-hater to exult. Until the season is over, there is no reason for me to give up—and the same is true for fans around the league. No matter how badly their team is doing, when the Yankees come to town it's a brand-new ballgame, and if they can beat the Yankees that day, that's all that matters.

A cheering crowd—and unlike the situation in some cities, the fans tonight were Indian fans, not transplanted or misplaced Yankee fans—can inspire the players, but the fans also take their cues from the players. If ballplayers are merely going through the motions, it is usually pretty obvious. But when the players are pumped up and want a win more than anything else, you have got to root for them with all your soul. And you had to feel happy tonight for Wayne Garland, who had been such a disappointment since Cleveland signed him as a free agent to a $2.3 million ten-year contract in 1976. His last year with Baltimore he was 20–7. Since then for Cleveland he has been 19–32. Tonight, however, he was masterful. And when he ended the game by getting Reggie to ground weakly into a doubleplay, catcher Bo Diaz greeted him with a hug that was so genuine, I wanted to squeeze the TV set, my Cleveland Indians wastebasket, or my wife—anything to join in that moment.

Friday, July 4. I see more than enough of Reggie Jackson on the playing field—even when he is reduced, as he has been lately, to the DH role. I definitely do not need to see more of him in between innings. But Reggie is popping up as the newest spokesman for Murjani Menswear. He was previously seen during commercial breaks as the spokesman for Panasonic's Reggie-vision, I mean Omnivision, a device that allows you to tape your swing when you're on the road for repeated viewings with your date when you're back in your pad. The Murjani ad assaults us with a new level of tackiness as Reggie stands next to a Porsche Targa in the vain hope that some of the car's class will rub off on his jeans. It is hard for blue jeans to look uncomfortable, but Reggie's do. Your next reaction is where did he get that ugly yellow pullover he is wearing with them. Reggie supplies the answer: the top is by Murjani, too. Reggie then supplies the purported explanation for the awful clothes he's wearing: "A guy's got an obligation to his fans," which is climactically inscribed in large type on the screen like it's the company motto, or a Confucian saying.

Reggie has to work hard, though, to keep ahead of his boss, George Steinbrenner, who appears between innings courtesy of SportsPhone and Colonial Franks: "C'mon, George, who've you signed?" "Gentlemen, we've re-signed a performer who's been consistently hot at the plate, Colonial Yankee Franks." George's Lite Beer commercial with Billy Martin has been retired, but when Billy was in town last month the two combatants spent a morning filming a commercial for Pepto-Bismol that will undoubtedly be with us shortly.

Speaking of Colonial, that's the company that hired for its commercials last year the only non-English-speaking Yankee, Luis Tiant. In one of the commercials, which has been carried over to this year, Louie's role consists of standing there, frying up some bacon while the announcer makes a few baseball puns, until he is asked, "Now isn't it time to wake up the family?" and Louie answers, in what could be English or Spanish, or for that matter French or Italian, "No." In Tiant's other commercial last year he got to speak a complete sentence: "Ees great to bee weeth a weener." For months I thought Tiant was referring to the Yankees (and by extension their sponsor, Colonial) and making a cruel comment on the team he had played with the previous eight years, the Red Sox. I was embarrassed that Tiant, one of the master craftsmen on the mound, one of the great comeback stories of our time and a former star for the Cleveland Indians, should be exploited on the air sounding like our night doorman. Then it dawned on me that this was an ethnic pun: not only was Colonial's ad agency not interested in brushing up the pitcher's pidgin English, they were making a joke out of it. The wiener company was taking a winner and using him as a hot dog.

Saturday, July 5. After Guidry and John, my dreams of a Cleveland sweep have been compromised to hopes for a series split. Willie Randolph won tonight's game with his 64th walk of the year, which leads the Yankees and, apparently, the entire American League. Why Randolph should walk at all is a mystery: his strike zone is not particularly small, he doesn't crowd the plate, he is not an intimidating hitter, and with the meat of the Yankee lineup following him, he is never in a position where the opposition wants to pitch around him. Most of the credit must go to Randolph's patience and a very good batting eye: the pitch he took in the third inning tonight, on a 3–2 count with nobody on and two outs, could not have been more than an inch below the strike zone, if it was a ball at all.

Randolph is getting much of the experts' credit for the Yankees' offensive success so far this year, just as leadoff hitter Mickey Rivers did on the Yankee pennant-winners of the late '70s. This may be more a mark of the experts' desire to appear sophisticated by bypassing the obvious heavyweights than an accurate assessment of Randolph's contribution. Rivers not only got on base, he did it in maddening ways; he was an aggravation that could upset an opposing team's equilibrium and single-handedly change the momentum of a game. But everything Randolph does—and I will not dispute his competence, if only because he comes from the same Pittsburgh Pirate second-baseman mold that over fifteen years produced Julian Javier, Dave Cash, Rennie Stennett and Randolph—he does quietly. That the base on balls is his newest weapon is appropriate. But oh, it is frustrating to watch because it seems so unnecessary.

Bobby Murcer—and speaking of frustrating, when are they going to bench this guy?—followed Randolph's walk with another home run. So on "Beat-the-Yankees Hankies" Night in Cleveland, both teams got four hits, including two home runs. But the only runner on base for any of the homers was Randolph, and the Yankees won 3–2.

Sunday, July 6. I have figured out how to beat the Yankees: Pitch your best lefthander against Ed Figueroa and when you make your move, make sure you get enough runs to last the game because it is the only shot you'll get. Howser starts Figgy out of some sense of duty and because with Tiant injured he's the only righthanded starter left on the staff, but Howser doesn't stay with him long. Today the hook came as soon as Figueroa gave up a hit in the sixth inning. It was not the point at which one would normally look to the bullpen, and Figgy showed he shared that view by throwing his glove at the dugout wall as he left the field. Indian manager Dave Garcia recognized the importance of the moment and lifted Rick Manning, the key to Cleveland's defense, in favor of power hitter Gary Alexander. Alexander, unbelievably in view of his .205 average, delivered his second pinch home run in a row, and the Indians took a 5–2 lead.

The last three innings were nervous time, as the Yankees chipped away at the lead. When Dent walked (can you stand it!) and Randolph singled with one out in the ninth, Garcia was faced, once again, with the choice of leaving in Rick Waits or going for Sid Monge in the bullpen. This time he made the move and looked very smart when Piniella hit the first pitch into a game-ending 6–4–3 doubleplay. The Tribe had shown the rest of the league how to play the Yankees even.

In fact, they came out ahead on the four games if I use the scoring technique my father has developed for his tennis matches: totals. He developed this system as a way of avoiding apparent ties in things like friendly mixed doubles games. For example, if he and my mother split sets with their neighbors, losing 6–4 then winning 6–3, they would emerge as the overall champions, 10–9. It's a good way of keeping one's incentive up for each game even when you're way ahead or behind. It is also a good way to ambush your opponents, who don't know you are scoring the match this way until it is over. Applied to a baseball series, this system gives significance to the seemingly meaningless four runs the Indians scored off Ron Davis on Friday, when they were losing 11–1. Those runs in a losing cause proved to be the difference in Cleveland's 19–17 totals triumph over the Yankees.

Monday, July 7. What a break! My wife's birthday falls this year on the day off before the All-Star Game. "No, sweetie," I can say, "I wouldn't think of watching a stupid old baseball game on your birthday. Let's go out for a four-course dinner and linger over coffee just as long as your heart desires." Then, since I've been such a sport about her birthday, she'll have to be more understanding on the few occasions between now and October when I may want to watch a little baseball on TV.

My wife acted as if she had made a discovery last week when she told me that one of her suburban friends, whom I'll call Joan, had complained that her husband would automatically turn on the TV when he came home from his law firm and relax in front of a ball game. Joan, who agrees with my wife on just about everything anyway, said she couldn't imagine anything more boring than watching baseball. The only surprise for me was that Joan's husband, whom I never took to be much of a sports fan, was actually just like hundreds of other guys I know. Every month, it seems, I hear of another non-sportsy male acquaintance who watched the ball game last night. And that almost always means there is another household where the wife can't understand what's going on.

I have explained to my wife that just because I am watching the ball game doesn't mean I can't talk to her, or listen to what happened to her at work that day. At first she would go crazy when right at the key point of her narrative I would turn my head slightly to watch a play at the plate. Now, as all good married couples must do, we have worked out a mode of living together in which she tells me all the routine news while the game is on but saves anything important for the pregame or postgame hours. Since on some nights none of these coincide with the hours she is awake, we sometimes put off talking things over, but there is usually plenty of time to catch up on the weekends. Still, it is nice to have two days between April 9 and October 5 on which there will be no baseball played, and even nicer that one of those two is my wife's birthday.

Tuesday, July 8. Let's put aside our prejudices and honor the members of the New York Yankees who played for the losing American League team in tonight's All-Star Game:

Bucky Dent—chosen by the fans as the top shortstop in the AL, he ranked a distant *eighth* in a quality-check straw poll of American League players conducted by the *Times,* getting only 4 votes as opposed to 148 for Robin Yount.

Willie Randolph—played seven innings, longest of anyone, which gave him time to make four bad plays in the field, including an error that allowed the winning run to score, and kill a rally by getting picked cleanly off first.

Tommy John—the master came home and gave up a homer to Griffey and three singles, for three earned runs and the All-Star loss.

Rich Gossage—after the heat of Richard and Welch, the

Goose looked tame; the first three batters clubbed line drives, but one was caught and one was foul.

Graig Nettles—threw out Lopes after a trademark dive, which wasn't really necessary, and was 0-for-2 at the plate.

Reggie Jackson—with checked-swing strikeout and half-swing single Reggie failed to dominate, or even affect the outcome; but as he said a few days ago, "I don't really go there to compete, I go there to be seen."

I suppose that hating the Yankees, combined with living in a city with two National League teams, helped make me a National League fan. When the leagues squared off in October, it was always the Yankees on one side and the National League on the other. The National League was always the underdog, as well, and this carried over to the All-Star Game: entering the '50s, the AL held a lopsided 12–4 edge. Yankee players also polluted the American League squad, but except for Mantle few had any memorable impact on the games. I have always regarded the All-Star Game, in fact, as a chance for the non-New York players to catch up on some national attention.

Tonight's game was short on the two categories I look for in All-Star play: elder statesmen and rising west-of-the-Hudson stars. Fred Lynn and Ken Griffey, who hit the only home runs, are both solidly in mid-career and have hardly been underexposed. Practically the only story in a dull mediocre game was formerly obscure Baltimore pitcher Steve Stone. A ten-year journeyman, Stone was named starting pitcher for the AL (albeit by his own manager), which prompted him to bestow thanks on all his teammates. When he retired nine National Leaguers in a row, the first pitcher in fourteen years to do so, he came off the mound beaming. It was almost enough to get me to root for the AL's second win since 1962. But that was only the third inning. As more Yankees became involved, I realized that I would hear about it for the rest of the year should TJ, Goose, Willie or, heaven forbid, Reggie lead the American League to victory. A loss might even, I said to myself, affect their confidence for the second half of the season or, failing that, in the World Series. And if the Yankees pretend that the All-Star Game doesn't produce any losers, I would refer them to Disneyland's hour of pregame ceremonies climaxed by Toni Tenille lip-synching, a full second late, "The Star-Spangled Banner."

Thursday, July 10. Does one's choice of ball team affect one's overall outlook on life? I mean only to raise the thought, not belabor the subject, as I examine the major league standings at the occasion of the All-Star break, traditionally the first time one is permitted to take seriously the relative positions of the contending teams. Having always been a Yankee-hater, I very early became a confirmed fatalist. I realized that, in the words of Doris Day then popular, what would be would be, and what would be most of the time was the Yankees. Rather than go around depressed, I accepted this as my lot and made my accommodation. If I had grown up in Chicago rooting for the Cubs, would I be more the eternal optimist? From Philadelphia or Boston would I be more the insecure zealot? And was I able to root for Cleveland and avoid a pessimistic outlook only because I wasn't living in Cleveland and reading of the Indians' travails every day?

Fatalism is easy when the Yankees hold a 7½-game lead at All-Star time. What will be, probably is already. If the Tigers were in first place and the Yankees fourth, then my fatalism would be a more remarkable quality, for I would be skillfully avoiding the "Is this the year of the Tiger?" hoopla that the media would be spewing forth. Reggie Jackson is trying to make it a little interesting by saying, "Hey, we can't play .670 ball the rest of the year" (as is his wont, slightly exaggerating the level of excellence involved), but I suspect that deep down all Reggie is concerned with for the rest of the season is winning the AL home-run crown and the Most Valuable Player Award.

Face it, as I have. The Yankees are unstoppable this year. Except for the starting pitching, they will be a much better team the second half of the season than they were in the first. Injuries to their two irreplaceable players is the only possible derailment that comes to mind, and I can't see Gossage and Cerone having it out in the shower. But being fatalistic, if the Yankees suddenly collapse, I think I can handle that, too.

Saturday, July 12. The Yankees, in another Steinbrenner departure from their tradition of aloof arrogance, have announced two fan contests which I am planning to enter. One is a simple raffle: send a card in and one name will be drawn from a hat on August 8. The prize is an all-expense-paid trip to California to watch the Yankees play three games against the Angels, August 22–24. If I win, I will pass up the Disneyland part of it, and also probably one of the games with the Angels, who have far and away the worst record in the majors this year. But even with the incredibly reduced air fares to California this summer, which, come to think of it, is probably how the Yankees got the idea, I couldn't pass up a free flight to the West Coast.

There is one other requirement: I have to name my "favorite Yankee." I could always use the old line, the only good Yankee is a dead Yankee, but that's probably a bit of overkill and for all I know might get me disqualified from the drawing. So I think I'll name Joe Lefebvre who, perhaps not coincidentally, has been a Yankee for a shorter period of time than anyone but Tim Lollar. He speaks well, has a good attitude, hustles, and makes the most of a less-than-awesome physique. And—subtle message here to Yankee management—he plays Reggie Jackson's position. With the exception of Reggie, there are no Yankees I personally dislike. In my view, Yankee-hatred is like anti-Americanism in the Arab world or a Communist country in that it is directed at the team itself, not at the individual players or citizens. It would even be possible, I suppose, to individually like all 25 players on the Yankee roster and still want the team to lose. I do happen to prefer some Yankees—Cerone and Watson, for instance—to others, but except for Lefebvre there is no one I would not want to see hit .200 for the year. Among the pitchers, I obviously prefer Guidry to Figueroa, which works out well because Guidry is so good that I never feel compelled to root for him. I am rooting for him in this popularity contest, though, because he has the only chance, however slight, to slow down a Reggie runaway. However transparent his obnoxious qualities may be, Reggie is in solid with the crowd that wants to go to Disneyland.

The second contest is more sophisticated, both in requirements and reward. Describe in two hundred words or less what position you would like to play in Yankee Stadium and why and you could be chosen, on literary merit not luck, to the George Plimpton All-Star team that will play two innings before a future Yankee home game. As one who at one stage or another of a less-than-illustrious career has played every position, which would I choose? First base, because it is the easiest? Pitcher, because it gets the most attention? Rightfield, because it is the least likely to have any action? Catcher, because it will receive the fewest applications? Third base, because my Yankee idol, Clete Boyer, played there? Centerfield, because in Yankee Stadium it is hallowed ground? Shortstop, because that is my current softball position? Or second base, because I would like uniform number 1? The only position with nothing going for it in Yankee Stadium is leftfield, which could be just reason enough to make that my selection.

Sunday, July 13. Sunday lunch at my parents' house today gave me the chance to ask my father, from whom I inherited my name, my love of baseball and most of my personality quirks, how he got started on Yankee-hating. His route, it turns out, was a well-traveled one, but that only makes it all the more worth repeating. Born and raised in Pittsburgh, he was fortunate to attend his first major league baseball game, at the age of seven, in a year that the Pirates won what would be their last world championship for 35 years. He went to the games with his grandfather, Thomas Marshall, Jr., his cousin Bud and some associates from his grandfather's law office—usually on holidays when the schedule had the Pirates playing morning and afternoon games (separate admissions) to make up for the Pennsylvania blue laws that prohibited baseball on Sunday. Dad's grandfather was a real fan, and he gave a famous luncheon party at his home before Opening Game each year, with a hurdy-gurdy on the front lawn. By contrast, Thomas Marshall III had passes to the Judges Box in Forbes Field but never used them or let his son, my father, use them, out of a concern for appearing prejudiced if a case involving the Pirates, or some injured spectator, should show up in his courtroom.

In 1927 my father got to go to his first World Series game. Unfortunately, the Pirates' opposition was a New York Yankee team that won a phenomenal 110 games that year, led by Babe Ruth's 60 home runs, Lou Gehrig's 175 runs batted in, Earle Combs's 231 hits and Waite Hoyt's 22 wins. Bob Meusel and Tony Lazzeri hit .337 and .309 and chipped in with 103 and 102 RBIs, respectively. The Pirates had added the Waner brothers, hitting .355 and .380, to the 1925 team that had beaten the Washington Senators. But the Yankees swept Pittsburgh, four games to zip. Over the course of the next twenty-three years, Yankee teams were to administer similar World Series shutouts to National League pennant winners from St. Louis, Chicago (twice), Cincinnati and Philadelphia, and thousands of other Yankee-haters were undoubtedly born. But in 1927 the Yankees were in Pittsburgh, making a lifelong enemy of my father.

The Pirates came close to winning once again before Dad left home—in 1938 when Gabby Hartnett's after-dark home run snatched away the pennant for the Cubs. The Cubs then lost four straight to a new Yankee team led by Bill Dickey,

Joe DiMaggio, Red Rolfe and pitchers Red Ruffing and Lefty Gomez. Three years later my father got to see a World Series game again: he sat behind the visitors' dugout at Ebbets Field and saw the Dodgers lose a game they should have won—to the Yankees. Tommy Henrich swung for a third strike with two outs in the ninth, but the pitch in the dirt got past catcher Mickey Owen, Henrich was safe at first, and the Yankees went on to score four runs for a 7–4 win. In 1950 Dad moved to New York, in time to catch the Yankees' five straight World Series wins, although the first he saw in person was in 1953 when Billy Martin, the worst hitter on the team, got 12 hits in the six-game triumph over the Dodgers.

My father remembers that he liked Gehrig ("everyone did"), thought of Ruth as a movie star, liked DiMaggio, admired Mantle because he could bunt and switch-hit as well as hit home runs, considered Rizzuto a fine shortstop and respected Howard as the Yankees' first black. The only player he remembers hating was Yogi Berra, for his facility at hitting home runs in the late innings of games the Yankees were about to lose. It was the Yankees as a team, the team that for forty-five years dominated baseball, that my father couldn't stand.

And after we finished talking, he went up to his room and turned on the TV—not to watch the team with the best midseason record (53–28) since the American League started playing 162 games a year, but to watch the Mets, trying once again to reach the .500 mark, 3½ games behind the Pirates.

Monday, July 14. Three frustrating losses in a row by the White Sox were almost enough to make me suspend my Yankee-watching. Saturday night was a study in Tommy John. The Yankees got a run in the first off another Randolph walk, and for eight innings John protected a 1–0 lead. The Chicago batters tried to wait out his low sinker by taking the first pitch, which was invariably a strike down the middle. Then John would nibble at the strike zone's lower corners. When the count reached 2–2 or 3–2, the batter expected a strike and swung—while the ball dipped unhittably down to ankle-height for another strikeout. The Yankees ultimately added a seven-run ninth off three relievers, but I quit in frustration before that, mourning a wasted pitching effort by Chicago's Ross Baumgarten.

Sunday afternoon the Hose hitters were even Paler, managing a grand total of two hits off Rudy May. But since they were a double and single good for a run, while the Yankees were being no-hit by Rainbow Trout, the game had possibilities. Even the White Sox can win a no-hitter, I assured myself. But in the eighth Trout walked Eric Soderholm on a 3–2 pitch, the tying run scored on a single by Ruppert Jones, and Rick Cerone finished off the Yankees' overwhelming three-hit attack with a home run to left for a 3–1 win.

Tonight's game again went down to the last two innings. In fact, it went down steadily from the end of the second, at which point the White Sox had somehow amassed a 6–1 lead. Another young lefty, Rich Wortham, was pitching for Chicago, striking out Reggie with sliders on the outside corner. But the Yankees got three runs in the sixth, and in the eighth Oscar Gamble came off the bench, watched three curves for a 1-2 count and creamed Ed Farmer's high fastball into the upper deck in right to tie the score. I still can't believe the Yankees won the game on Reggie's baserunning, but when I got out of the shower they were showing a replay of Reggie's ninth-inning hookslide around the catcher and saying he had stolen second base to set up Spencer's winning pinch hit. I watched the bottom of the ninth out of sheer masochism. The leadoff man hit a freak single—then was out stealing when the Sox tried a hit-and-run on a Gossage fastball. Reggie, who has played rightfield the last week like he thought it would bite him, deflected a two-out single by Chet Lemon past Ruppert Jones and Lemon made it to third, where he and I watched Hal Baines fan to end my agony and the three-game series.

Tuesday, July 15. Reflections on a Tuesday night game in July:

Nothing brings out the fans like a winner. I have never seen lines fifty-people long at every ticket window, but that's what I am waiting in to get to see the Yankees play a mediocre, starless Twins team. On the other hand, it is the first home game in two weeks, Guidry is pitching against ex-Met Jerry Koosman, and the only thing on TV is the Republican Convention.

If most of the 30,000 fans, like me, bought their tickets at the gate, all of them *except* me are here to see Guidry strike out every Twin who comes to the plate. I think I have walked into the lions' den when the Minnesota leadoff batter, Bombo Rivera, strikes out amid a crescendo of rhythmic clapping and other signs of mass hysteria.

How to ruin an evening early: Reggie slices a 3–0 pitch high into the air and ultimately the leftfield stands for a 3–0 first-inning lead. Bows and cap-tipping all around, many waves to the fans in right as Reggie comes out to start the second inning.

The sound of peanuts being cracked all around me after the peanut vendor passes by in the fourth inning is a comforting rustling noise, unique to the ballpark, that makes me contented to be in the last box in section 17 on a sultry evening, even if the Yankees are still winning, 3–2.

On one side of me is a 60-year-old man, probably an accountant or a postal clerk, with gray glasses, a green short-sleeved shirt and a demure white-haired wife. He cheers every play in a voice raised higher than it ever goes at work or home, but still barely audible five feet away. For whom is he making these noises—"That's a hit, attaboy Bucky," "Ce-rone, Ce-rone, Ce-rone!" "Come on Dennis, don't strike out again"? Not the players or those of us sitting near him. Certainly not his wife, who has little idea what is going on.

What does a first-base coach—in the case of the Twins someone named Karl Kuehl—do? He doesn't give signs or tell the runner, who can see as well as he can, to take an extra base. Is his position vestigial, or perhaps merely symmetrical?

I am happily on my third beer. The two couples in front of me are passing a joint down the line. Behind me is a middle-aged father with his three middle-aged sons, who discuss the players' salaries. At least the youngest, who looks about 13, has his glove with him.

What is Reggie eating in rightfield from his hip pocket between batters? Not spinach for his fielding, for his error contributes to two Twin runs and their first lead, 4–3.

Willie Randolph, the walking wonder, does his thing on four pitches, Koosman's only unintentional walk of the game. Then in the seventh inning, when I concentrate on convincing Koosman not to walk him, Randolph hits a surprise home run to left, erasing the Twins' short-lived lead.

The scoreboard tells us that Ken Clay lost a game for Columbus yesterday. Remember him?

The Twins retake the lead, 5–4, on a suicide squeeze, a daring call against Gossage. Even Yankee fans, I think, appreciate the beautifully executed play. The Minnesota runs have been driven in by people named Edwards, Wilfong, Butera, Castino and Cubbage. The Twins All-Star hitter Landreaux has not hit a ball out of the infield and leadoff hitter Rivera has lived up to his first name, striking out three times in a row.

Between innings, the organist plays a tune and always skillfully segues into "I Love New York," which may be the shortest song ever written and makes "Happy Birthday" sound long and varied in comparison.

With a man on second and no outs, Reggie hits a soft grounder to second and claps for himself as he runs toward first. He is trying to fool somebody (Rizzuto?) into thinking that all he wanted to do was move the runner along, but I am Reggie-proof.

Howser's insistence on sticking with a righthanded DH,

even when rookie Dennis Werth is the only righthander available, reveals a rookie manager's weakness: he sticks too closely to the book. Surely Murcer or Gamble would have done better against a wily veteran pitcher than the doubleplay grounder and three strikeouts Werth produced, the last two with men in scoring position.

Can't the Yankees go down quietly in the ninth just once, for me? Jones hits a leadoff single—good game, Kooz—and advances to third with two outs.

How many times have you seen a *shortstop* barehand a slow grounder and throw to first in one motion, like a third baseman playing a bunt? The Twins' Pete Mackanin does it to get Randolph, and win for the Twins this game of inches.

Thursday, July 17. Welcome to Cosmos Country. At least, I feel welcome today when I can read of the Cosmos' second straight loss and can avoid lingering on the Yankees' routine 10–1 rout of the Twins.

The Cosmos are a parody of the Yankees, and I don't mean just because they are going for their third championship in four years. Start with a free-spending ownership, which has paid millions in the free-agent market to import such international superstars as Pele, Beckenbauer, and Chinaglia. Not selected ones, but two or three for every position on the field. They also have a farm system of the best American young players, none of whom may ever make it to the parent squad. The other similarity in the player-acquisition program is that the owner does not seem to consult with the coach before he makes his acquisitions. If someone has a big enough reputation, get him, regardless of whether the Cosmos need someone at his position. So what if they already have five lefthanded-hitting utility outfielders for pinch hitting?

Then there is the meddling by ownership. The Cosmos' management last year imported a flashy blonde from Brazil named Marinho, who in some games took more shots than the rest of the team put together, even though he played midfield.

Much like Billy Martin with Reggie, the Cosmos' coach benched Marinho to try to restore some semblance of team play on the field, which strategy lasted only until the coach was fired. This year the Cosmos have their fifth coach in four years, slightly unusual for a team that has been in first place for the entire time.

Finally, there are the players, whose resemblance to the Yankees is uncanny but perhaps not coincidental. Maybe by being in New York they learn how American sports stars are supposed to behave by reading about the Yankees. Maybe it's the press's fault, because they look for the same things their colleagues are covering on the Yankees. Or maybe signing a million-dollar contract just does something to an athlete. Anyway, the whole season is filled with play-me-or-trade-me quotes, injuries being feigned by players or fabricated by management, sullen athletes skipping practice or missing flights and headlined incidents having nothing to do with the sport at hand—like last year's brawl between three Cosmos and the crew that was sweeping out the stadium after a game.

But still, the greatest and worst similarity is that they win practically all the time.

Friday, July 18. What better sendoff for our summer vacation trip to the South and Midwest than to see the Kansas City Royals pulverize the Yankees tonight, 13–1. Going into the bottom of the ninth, Kansas City was outhitting New York 21–1, and the crowd of 50,000 was in constant motion toward the exits. We will be visiting Tennessee and St. Louis first, before we arrive with the Yankees in Kansas City next Friday. Until then, I will savor Larry Gura's three-hitter, Willie Wilson's five hits and devastating delayed steal of second and one more dominating hitting performance by the fabulous George Brett. Needing one uplifting play to show during the credits at game's end, Channel 11 replayed Willie Randolph's leaping catch of a line drive—the only time the Yankees got Brett out all night.

Chapter 6
THE VIEW FROM
THE MIDWEST
Road Trip!

Saturday, July 19. "Down on the Farm" is now a regular feature of Yankee promotion: the scoreboard in Yankee Stadium gives a report once a night on the Yankee minor league teams, and Healy and Messer, the semiofficial company shills, give reminders on the radio broadcast that Yankee superiority extends all the way down to Class A.

Down on the farm is also where my favorite Yankee, Joe Lefebvre, is playing now, along with such one-time Yankees as Brian Doyle, Mike Griffin, Ken Clay, Dennis Sherrill, Bruce Robinson and Roy Staiger. Lefebvre went down to Columbus (Ohio) with some classy the-team-comes-first quotes, a victim of By-the-Book Howser's feeling he should have another righthanded hitter to platoon with.

And down on the farm, one level below Triple-A Columbus, is where I went yesterday, as we flew from 95-degree New York City to 105-degree Nashville. My aunt Jennie met us at the airport and we drove to see Andrew Jackson's home, the Hermitage, the vast parking lot for Opryland, U.S.A., historic Belle Meade Mansion, Vanderbilt University, and, as the sun was finally setting, Greer Stadium, home of the Nashville Sounds.

The Sounds are the Yankees' Double-A farm team and are known in New York mainly for their 23-year-old first baseman, Steve Balboni, whom Messer has adopted as his personal booster project. "My man Steve Balboni hit another home run last night," Messer is fond of telling us in a lull in the Yankee game. You would think that Rizzuto, who is fixated on every Italian surname that writes in with a birthday message, would have been the one to adopt Balboni, but since he seemingly spends every nonworking minute on some golf course, he is dependent on Messer and White for all news of what's happening in the rest of the world, let alone in the minor leagues.

All box and reserve seats for the Saturday night game with the Orlando Twins had been sold a week in advance, but sitting in the bleachers behind third, we still felt closer to home plate than I can remember ever being at Yankee Stadium. The electric scoreboard alternately flashed the time and the temperature—it started at 96° and went down one degree each inning—and in big block letters the name and position of each player as he came to bat. Maybe because it was Jacket Night—my wife thinks it is always Jacket Night—there were thousands of kids in the five-to-twelve year range, and the crowd was constantly in motion. People coming, going, with sno-cones, pizzas and ice-cream helmets. When the announcer wasn't leading cheers—"Number fourteen, the DH, Ken-neee BA-ker!"—he was giving away door prizes by seat number, ticket number and best guess of the evening's attendance, and by the seventeen lucky numbers printed in each 75¢ Souvenir Program—"Dinner for two at Captain D's for Lucky Number 29348."

The field itself, like every baseball field, was beautiful. The foul poles were 330 feet from home, there was a 405-foot sign in center, and at 375 Balboni's power alley in left-center was the only distance notably shorter here than in Yankee

Stadium. There were no stands, just an emptiness, behind the outfield fence with its 56 commercial advertisements. A half-moon soon replaced the sunset-pink clouds, and a large lighted billboard for Cutty Sark, about a half mile away, loomed over the rightfield wall. The players wore bright red jerseys and looked more like the Cleveland Indians than a Yankee affiliate. Some of their names, in addition to Balboni, were vaguely familiar from spring training box scores, like Buck Showalter in left field and pitcher Dan Ledduke. Catcher Brad Gulden had even played in 40 games with New York last year after Munson's death.

The Sounds broke the ice with two runs in the third on singles by Baker, Balboni and Garry Smith, with a walk to Gulden in between. The Twins took the lead on four runs in the next inning, the key blow a line drive off pitcher Ledduke's right ankle, after which he got nobody out but the manager. But the Sounds immediately answered. Andre Robertson, a quick and fluid black shortstop who had caught my scout's eye, led off with a single. I was ready to check his base-stealing speed when he pulled one better: when the second baseman tried to tag him on a routine doubleplay grounder, he reversed fields and headed back to first so quickly that no tag was made. The flustered fielder then threw too late to first to catch the batter and Robertson turned again and cruised into second. From there Showalter tied the game with an opposite-field double, Baker drove in Showalter, and the crowd joined the announcer in yelling, "Steve Bal-boni!" From his closed stance, our man waited on the second pitch, uncoiled and pulled the ball over the wall by the scoreboard, 360 feet away.

Maybe it wouldn't have made it in Yankee Stadium, but down on the farm it was good for a 7–4 lead. Balboni had increased his home run total to 28 (four more than Reggie Jackson), destroyed for the night the chances of Orlando (the final score was 11–5), and put a storybook, if not a country-and-western, ending on a New Yorker's visit to the minor leagues. I have never left a game so early, but the four innings had taken an hour and a half and there were no backs on our bleacher seats. It hardly mattered who won—and even though we had flown 700 miles to get to the ballpark, we still had another 100 miles to drive before we could sleep.

Sunday, July 20. The Nashville Sounds are leading their league by five games, which is not unusual for a Yankee farm club these days. When the Yankees were having such a bad year in 1979, Yankee apologists routinely pointed out that the minor league teams were winning big and that help was on the way. My answer was that of course the Yankees had the best 24-year-olds in the minor leagues, because the best 24-year-olds belonging to other teams were already in the majors!

Last May, when Howser was using Griffin, Lefebvre, Brown and Werth, the word was passed around that Steinbrenner's success formula had moved from Stage 1, the acquisition of expensive free agents, to Stage 2, harvesting the fruits of the best farm system money could buy. With the return of Jones and Gamble, all talk of fruits has suddenly subsided.

Will the husky Balboni, to take one example, grow up to be a Yankee? With both Spencer and Watson well on the wrong side of 30, New York may need a new first baseman in a couple of years. But Balboni, like almost any rookie, will take some developing, and if there is anything that George Steinbrenner has less of than class, it is probably patience. And why should he wait on some youngster when he is so good at filling holes with proven big-leaguers? Look at Chambliss, look at Watson. In two years such possible acquisitions as Seattle's Bruce Bochte and Chicago's Lamar Johnson will be a ripe 31 and Oakland's Dave Revering 29, four years younger than Watson was when he played his first game as a Yankee. I predict that Balboni will eventually play in Yankee Stadium and that I'll be rooting for him—because he won't be playing for the Yankees.

Monday, July 21. I had known that I wouldn't be leaving the Yankees behind when the lady across the aisle in the airplane asked the steward if we could fly over Yankee Stadium on our way to Nashville. We flew over Brooklyn instead.

Sure enough, there in the Nashville and Chattanooga sports sections this morning were articles not only on the Royals' 14–3 drubbing of the Yanks, but on our old friends Ed Figueroa and Billy Martin. Of Kansas City's 54 hits in the three-game series (New York won Saturday, 13–7), 13 were off Figgy, who pitched five innings in relief. "I can't get any better coming in from the bullpen like that, no way." Since Figgy has so far had one good game all year, and that was when the Oakland hitters were sleepwalking, he has lots of room to get better in. The question is how much time.

Billy is back with excerpts from *Number One,* a book he is "co-authoring" with a writer named Peter Golenbock. The "news" is Billy's charge that George Steinbrenner reneged on promises, pitted Billy against Reggie, and meddled with the club. These allegations can't really be considered news, even in Chattanooga. The final charge is that George tapped the manager's phone, which brought an offer to resign, if true, from the stadium manager in charge of all phone taps. The real news in the story for me was the disclosure of how Billy's book was being written. Golenbock is the penstriped amanuensis who brought us Sparky Lyle's *Bronx Zoo,* not to mention *Guidry* and *Dynasty.* His co-author on this one handled yesterday's controversy by complaining: "I never reviewed the manuscript in its final form as per the original agreement I entered into with the author and publisher, so I am not in a position to comment about the book at this time."

Because he was too busy changing pitchers in Oakland? Because the co-author didn't want him to see the sensational stories he was slipping in to boost sales? Because his "gentleman's agreement" with Steinbrenner won't let him be a party any longer to critical comments about his former boss, who is presumably still paying him off? Because he can't read? I can already see the post-publication interview on Merv Griffin: "Billy, how were you able to tell your life story so candidly?" "Gee, Merv, I don't know. I haven't read it yet."

Tuesday, July 22. News bulletin on Tennessee TV: The Yankees have announced that Ed Figueroa will be traded or released to make room for Luis Tiant, returning from the disabled list:

> *Good-bye Figgy,*
> *Good-bye Figgy,*
> *Good-bye Figgy,*
> *We hate to see you go.*

Or perhaps, we should celebrate:

> *Now bring us some Figgy pudding . . .*

Wednesday, July 23. We arrived in St. Louis, Missouri, home of the *Sporting News,* the same day that publication put Reggie Jackson—"Peace at Last"—on its cover. I bought it anyway.

The article itself, mostly quotes from Jim Spencer, contributes to the new consensus view of Reggie as a man basking in his glory instead of, as he did formerly, suffering as the misunderstood, misused and unjustly maligned black man. The reasons for this change are not hard to find:

1. With Munson gone, not to mention such other old-timers as Chambliss, White, Hunter, Rivers and Lyle, Reggie has no competition for his claimed position as team leader.

2. With Billy Martin gone, Reggie has no competition for the fans' affections and the media's attention, both of which he desperately needs.

3. With the Yankees on the way to a division title and Reggie on the way to a home-run crown, the Yankees are in the spotlight and Reggie will have to be considered for the MVP Award.

4. With Reggie in his fourteenth season, his career stats are mounting and every week brings the record-conscious Reggie to some new "milestone."

5. On the horizon, Reggie can see two MVP Awards under his belt, five World Series rings on his fingers, other lifetime stats piled up on his broad shoulders, and somebody starting to take seriously Reggie's campaign for the Hall of Fame.

The one place where Spencer used his first-baseman's stretch was in evaluating Reggie's defense: "Now the fans have come to accept that while he's not the greatest outfielder, he's trying, really trying. I've never seen him not try to go after a ball." If he means he's never seen Reggie stand absolutely still on a ball hit to right, I suppose there's no argument.

Saturday, July 26. Everything's up-to-date in Kansas City, and nothing is in a more advanced stage than the Kansas Citians' Yankee-hating. All three games this weekend are advance sellouts, and the *front page* of this morning's *Kansas City Times* had an article describing last night's crowd as "otherwise mild-mannered Midwesterners out for East-Coast blood." " 'You want me to tell you why I hate the Yankees?' said 12-year-old Mike Knowles of Jefferson City. 'They're a bunch of phonies, that's why—like Reggie Jackson saying he's the best player in the league and never backing it up.' " Now I don't know that Reggie ever said such a thing, but 12-year-old Mike believed it as surely as the Soviet citizens believe Carter invented Afghanistan in order to sabotage the Olympics. And listen to Mike's official source of information: "Even more vehement was Mike's gray-haired grandmother, Lura Knowles. 'When you buy the pennant, you're hitting below the belt. Is that all there is to American society—win, win, win? If you have to cheat to win, you don't deserve it.' "

To observe this phenomenon at close hand, we ventured out last night with a local sports fan and his ballet-loving wife to Royals Stadium. It hadn't rained in Missouri for six weeks, but it started raining when we got out of the car in parking section F24, a good half mile from Royals Stadium, and it continued through the sixth inning. Not enough to delay the game. Just enough to send our wives in search of cover, to raise umbrellas in our line of vision, and to make the Yankee outfielders look particularly inept on the slick TartanTurf field.

Oscar Gamble imitated a DH playing rightfield in the second inning, giving Duke Wathan a single and Clint Hurdle, easily the slowest man in the Kansas City lineup, an inside-the-park home run. The next inning Bucky Dent backed off and let the charging Bobby Murcer drop a Texas Leaguer by U. L. Washington for a double, leading to the third run. The fourth got on base when Dent dribbled a ground ball, and it scored on a Brett triple that Murcer again misplayed. In the sixth Murcer watched an Aikens line drive skid past him to the wall. Wathan singled and stole second, and star-of-the-game Hurdle delivered both with a broken-bat single to left.

The only Yankee to make his presence felt was Reggie Jackson. Even though he was only DH'ing, Reggie was still out in center, taking one more warm-up lap, when the Royals took the field to start the game. And with two out and nobody on in the sixth and the Yankees losing 4–0, I told my friend that this was a spot for a Reggie goner—and it went on the next pitch for the only Yankee run in an eventual 6–1 defeat.

Although today's paper said "for Kansas City the crowd was very loud indeed," by New York standards it was a quiet evening in the rain. I realized just how subdued I had been when in the sixth inning the three cowboys from Wichita, Kansas, sitting behind us leaned over their beers and demanded, "Where y'all from—I don't see you cheering anybody." The thought flashed through my mind that signs at the gate said no cans or bottles allowed into the stadium, but said nothing about six-guns, and I quickly responded, "I'm from New York, but I just clapped for Hurdle." Then I thought, when was the last time I went to the ballpark, saw the Yankees lose and "just clapped"?

Sunday, July 27. Only for the Yankees, I was told, would there be those one hundred people standing on the hill beyond the outfield fence, watching the visitors take extra batting practice four hours before game time. And it was Brian Doyle and Chicken Stanley, not Reggie or Graig, who were doing the hitting. And there I was, not outside but in, standing next to a stone-faced Eric Soderholm as Stanley fouled another one of coach Jeff Torborg's pitches into the batting cage. So many things are easier to do in a small city like Kansas City, and penetrating the Yankee clubhouse was one of them. I know only four people in this city, but one is the boyfriend of the sister of the visiting team clubhouse manager, and he and I decided to revive our law school friendship by driving out together for an inside look at Royals Stadium.

Tom, the clubhouse manager, met Ed and me at the players' door, where another twenty-five youngsters were watching for their heroes to arrive and maybe pick up an autograph. He took us down to the blue-carpeted locker room, which he runs as a private concession from the Royals. It is his job to supply each visiting ball club with a tidy locker room stocked with free soft drinks, candy, chewing tobacco and after the game, beer and a buffet supper. In return for the food and the countless errands Tom and his teenage staff run, each player gives Tom a tip when the series is over. The job also involves a lot of sitting around, which is what Ed and I were helping Tom with this afternoon. It was only 3:30, and the team bus had not yet arrived. But Piniella and Guidry and the outgoing Ron Davis were sitting at a card table playing a bridge-deviation called Pluck; Watson, Stanley and a left-handed pitcher wearing number 59 were getting dressed; and Yogi Berra, even more leathery-faced in person than on TV, was milling around like a walking monument.

I wanted to feel the TartanTurf under my feet, so Tom took us down the short runway to the dugout, where Yankee superscout Bob Lemon was sitting in solitude, and onto the field. The sun was hot and the field was, as its name indicates, artificial. The surroundings, if not artificial, were expansively Midwestern. Looking out from home plate, there were no buildings in the distance, no stands in centerfield, no upper deck in right or left. Instead there was open space, except for the twelve-story-high scoreboard that illustrates the National Anthem lyrics before the game, resembles a pinball machine as it flashes a clutter of data during the game, and sings Coors Beer commercials between innings.

As the bronzed, good-looking Piniella entered the batting cage, my fantasies started to overwhelm me—with only three people in the field, surely they'd let me at least shag flies—and I figured we had better return to a more familiar reality. As we passed back through the locker room, Luis Tiant had arrived, a loudmouthed *New York Post* reporter was running around, and the ribbing was beginning in earnest. Didn't I want to stay and see the rest of the team and, as one of Tom's helpers said, the real "traveling circus" they attract?

In thirty-four years, this was the first time I had seen major-leaguers up close. Already my perspective had changed, for example, on Soderholm (for the worse) and Davis (for the better). If I now began to think of the Yankees as real people, what would happen to the Yankees I knew through baseball cards, through television, through newspaper articles, and through my binoculars from the upper deck of Yankee Stadium? No, baseball and Yankee-hating were too important to me. I had to get out of there.

Monday, July 28. The Tommy John half of the anticipated pitchers' duel misfired yesterday and the Royals scored an easy 8–0 win, giving Larry Gura a lifetime 7–1 mark against the Yankees and giving Kansas City a convincing 8–4 split of its regular season games with New York. You would think Kansas Citians would be going wild, or at least chanting "We're number one!" But the memory of regular-season wins followed by playoff losses to the Yankees in 1976, 1977 and 1978 hangs over this city as palpably as the Civil War defeat by another team of Yankees lingers in the consciousness of the South, and nothing will efface it short of a victory over New York this October. The worst memory is 1977, because the final loss came in Kansas City and it was over a Royal team that had led the majors with 102 wins and is still regarded as the best team in Kansas City history. They won the first game and were never behind, until the ninth inning of the fifth game. Then they lost. End of season. Good-bye, World Series.

"We saw it coming—everyone in the stadium sensed it coming," recalled one man we met at a dinner party. "Herzog panicked. He brought in Dennis Leonard, who hadn't pitched in relief all year. When the Yankees went ahead, the whole season collapsed. Forget the bottom of the ninth. Everybody knew it was over. We staggered out to the parking lot. Cars weren't moving. I saw one man sitting in his car slamming his fist into the wheel. My wife and I just sat there and finished off the wine and cognac. For two hours. When we finally left, plenty of cars were still there."

The ball team means a lot to Kansas City. Like other smaller cities, the baseball and football teams are the city's tickets to equality with the most famous places in the country, and they are supported as a civic enterprise across the social spectrum. But in baseball, Kansas City has had some tough luck. Their first team, the ex–Philadelphia Athletics, finished sixth in 1955, their first year in Kansas City, and never did so well again. The Kansas City Athletics were famous mostly for supplying players to the New York Yankees. Maybe these trades were good for both teams, but the Yankees always won the pennant with ex-Athletics while the A's generally finished in the cellar. Having just reached the age where I had learned that pro wrestling was fixed, I had to wonder about this relationship as well.

The next blow to Kansas City pride was the 1967 departure of the entire team to Oakland, leaving Kansas City to start from scratch with an expansion franchise two years later. The new club, the Royals, took only three years to bloom, but for five years they couldn't dislodge their suddenly successful predecessors, the traitorous A's, from first place. Then in 1976 Oakland disbanded and the Royals' young collection of homegrown and skillfully traded players rose to dominance in the American League West. Kansas City awaited the national spotlight—only to find all attention diverted to New York, where George Steinbrenner had assembled the best team money could buy. For three years in a row they ran up against the Yankees in the Playoffs and failed; the last time they were licked before they even started.

By any objective or critical measure, the Royals have the best team in baseball in 1980. But their fans are not celebrating just yet. They still have a ghost that must be exorcised. And it's wearing a pinstripe uniform.

Saturday, August 2. We first heard about it from a cabbie one year ago today: "New York lost quite a ballplayer." I asked him if he meant Mickey Rivers, who had just been traded to Texas. "No, Munson," he said. "Munson was killed in a plane crash."

Several years ago Thurman Munson was my favorite Yankee-hating target. For one thing, he was extremely popular with the fans at Yankee Stadium. For another, he was a clutch hitter and did untold damage to my dreams of Yankee disaster. Finally, in my role as baseball expert I sincerely believed that Munson was not as good as Boston's Carlton Fisk, while Munson clearly believed that he was. I loved to point out Munson's sidearm throws that tailed away from second. Yet he somehow managed to throw most people out.

Four things markedly changed my attitude toward Munson. First was the arrival of Reggie in 1977, accompanied by his infamous remark, "I'm the straw that stirs the drink . . . Munson can only stir it bad." If a battle line was being drawn with Jackson on one side and Munson on the other, my support went to Thurman. Second, Munson began saying he wanted to be traded to Cleveland. Not only did I appreciate this disaffection with the Yankees, and Steinbrenner in particular, I had to like someone who actually *wanted* to play for the Indians. And Munson's willingness to go from a World Champion team to an also-ran was a refreshing contrast to the normal spoiled veteran who does not think baseball is fun unless he is playing with a "contender." Third, Munson's uncanny success in clutch situations began to noticeably decline after the 1977 season, making him less of a threat to my personal happiness.

The keystone to my arching respect, however, was his appearance in a Williams Lectric Shave commercial, the first time I had been exposed to the lighter side of this seeming grouch. He is called in to what pretends to be the owner's office to be dressed down—not for his play ("I'm doing a good job," he protests in advance), but for his beard. After being advised that Lectric Shave will allow him to get rid of his five o'clock shadow, Munson adjures, "Now I won't just be the best catcher . . . I'll be the best looking one, too." This charade (Munson possessed notably unglamorous features, unless your standard was Yogi Berra) lasts until he reaches the door, at which point he turns around and impishly appends, "Well, one of the best."

When Munson's plane crashed, the Yankees' 1979 season, already a bust, was completely written off by the media, who pushed the affair even further with comments to the effect of "How unimportant the game against the Orioles, or the American League pennant race, or even baseball itself, seem in the light of such a tragedy." That sentiment, which threatened to depress the entire summer, was no doubt well intended, but to my mind it missed the point. People die by the thousands every day—and many of the deaths are just as tragic and many take away people who are just as fine as Munson—but we hear of none of them. We knew of Munson, and his death, because of baseball, because of the American League pennant race, because of the series against the Orioles. Take them away and what would we have felt on Munson's death—if we had even heard of it?

I do not want to detract from the sadness all baseball fans felt at the loss of someone who, after all, was a part of our lives, the compassion we felt for his family, or the emotion we shared with the Stadium crowd that honored his memory with an eight-minute standing ovation. But, I believe, we should recognize that these feelings existed in us *because* of baseball, not in spite of it, and we need not feel guilty for allowing, even wanting, the show to go on.

Sunday, August 3. Eager to ascertain the pulse of New York upon returning from my two-week road trip, I made a comment on the Yankees to the welcoming doorman. "Aah, Bob," Jimmy replied, "I'm bored with baseball. I don't even watch the games anymore." Considering that the alternative is watching the street, that's a pretty severe position. Of course, no one ever said that winning all the time wasn't boring. And since monotonous victories have long been a hallmark of Yankee baseball, it is not surprising that these dog-day games have been boring, boring, boring.

When the Yanks are playing anyone except Kansas City, Boston or Baltimore, the opposition expects to lose, the Yankees expect to win and no one is terribly surprised or excited when that happens. Nor do the Yankees get excited when it doesn't happen, because they know they have won or will win the other two games in the series. Then there is the nature of the team. Now that Howser's rookie experiment is over, the Yankee lineup is dominated by veterans who have outlived emotional highs and lows and know better than to get worked up over a game in August. Nor do the players share their emotions. The obvious distance that separates Reggie from his teammates sets the tone for the relationships among this collection of individuals, each intent on his own performance.

The games themselves, from an aesthetic viewpoint, are often boring. When the Yankees lose, they are usually out of it early and simply go through the motions the rest of the way. And once they get ahead in the late innings, all semblance of contest is over. I don't know if there are statistics to back up my impression that the Yankees lead the majors in games decided by the seventh inning, but the fact that Goose Gossage sustained his first loss of the year last Wednesday says something. And the Yankees' preference for home runs as a method of attack, over triples, constructed rallies and strategy, also keeps the spectator excitement level down. The key contribution to the boredom, however, comes from the lack of quality opposition. Literally half the Yankee games are against second-rate teams—California, Seattle, Oakland, Toronto, Chicago and Minnesota come instantly to mind—and no one they face is involved in a pennant race.

Jimmy's observation came to mind last night when I watched the Yankees beat the Milwaukee Brewers for the third straight time, 5–3. On paper, the Brewers looked like the team to beat in the East this year, but when the Yankees arrived in town Thursday, after losing the series both in Kansas City *and* Minnesota, the Brewers were still eight games off the pace. Then instead of sweeping the Yankees to finally create a pennant race, the Brewers fell apart. Ahead 6–1 on Thursday, they lost when Reggie hit a three-run homer in the ninth and, if you can stand it, their catcher neglected to tag a runner coming home in the eleventh.

The Yankees put away the Friday night game with seven runs in the first inning. On Saturday the Brewers squandered a 3–0 lead with four errors good for five unearned runs. Even worse than the errors was a Soderholm "double" in the sixth with two outs and the bases loaded. Leftfielder Ben Oglivie lost the eminently catchable line drive in the lights, then saw it bounce off his glove and roll to the wall, clearing the bases. There was no life in the Brewers' mugs after that. Beyond not having a climax, the game was dull and poorly played. The outcome was predictable. The Brewers will play the Yankees again today, and it hardly matters now who wins or loses. Although it is only the third of August, this is the last game of 1980 between Milwaukee and New York. The Brewers' season might as well be over. My TV, like Jimmy's, will be off.

Chapter 7
THE ORIOLES
COME ON STRONG
So Does George

Wednesday, August 6. This has been a week of anticipation as two groups of Yankees point toward two different events this weekend. One group consists of Reggie Jackson, who is looking for his lifetime 400th home run. The other is the remainder of the team, who are preparing to face second-place Baltimore in what may be the only showdown of the 1980 American League season.

The concern over the red-hot Orioles, who are suddenly only five games behind New York in the loss column, is clearest in the juggling of the pitching rotation—to no one's particular pleasure, incidentally. The post-Figueroa rotation the Yankees have been using would turn up May, Tiant and Underwood to pitch against the Birds. But Underwood has been relegated to the bullpen in favor of John, who despite his customary second-half swoon that no one but me seems to have noticed has a 15–5 record. And May, who is 3–13 lifetime against Baltimore, was flopped with Guidry, who is in a slump but who is 5–1 lifetime against the Orioles. And Steinbrenner, recognizing that the stretch run this year is not in

September but in the next ten days, has acquired veteran third baseman Aurelio Rodriguez from the San Diego Padres for $100,000. A career .239 hitter, Rodriguez is insurance for sore-kneed Eric Soderholm, who was insurance for Graig Nettles, who is out indefinitely with hepatitis. Of course, .239 is 16 points better than the lifetime average of the all-risk policy the Yankees have carried for many years, Chicken Stanley.

As for the big man, he did say a couple of days ago: "First comes first. We're in a pennant race and we have to win the game before I worry about personal statistics." At the same time, he has made sure that no one can overlook the personal statistics by inviting his father, the retired tailor, to watch in the stands until he hits Number 400. He has also announced that he will give the ball to his father—can you think of a better place for Reggie to keep it?—and Panasonic is helping him get the ball by offering a 23-inch TV to the fan who retrieves it from the stands. The press is comparing the event to Maris's 61st, Aaron's 715th and Yaz's 3,000th hit, with no complaint from Reggie.

However you look at it—unless you want to point out that Harmon Killebrew hit 573 home runs with one-tenth of the publicity—Reggie's next home run will be a milestone or, as he says, "a summation of things." Which may, after all, relate to the upcoming Baltimore series and the fact that Jackson failed to hit Number 400 in the last two games with Texas. Why, tonight's game, a rather meaningless encounter in which Reggie went 0-for-4, wasn't even on TV! Every actor needs a stage and an audience. And what better way for Reggie to upstage the entire pennant race than to save his 400th tater until Baltimore gets to town.

Friday, August 8. The Orioles beat the Yankees 5–2 in the series opener in New York, the game that could set the tone for the two that follow, and maybe the five in Baltimore next week. And I now think that Baltimore has a shot at the lead because they, unlike the Yankees, are "tournament tough."

The Yankees have piled up wins against not very good opposition, and with their huge lead, they have not been in any "must" games this year. The Orioles have been as far as 11 games behind the Yankees. Every game they have played since the All-Star break has been crucial to their hopes to get back in a pennant race. They also went through the pennant race, Playoffs and World Series last year. The Yankees haven't been in a pennant race since 1978, and 40 percent of the current team wasn't here then.

How does this lack of tournament toughness manifest itself on the diamond? In the failure to come up with the big play. Tonight we saw it in Ruppert Jones, who is playing in his first big series. In fairness, Jones's home run gave the Yankees a temporary 2–1 lead in the seventh. But in the top of the eighth, Baltimore tied the game on Eddie Murray's home run and put runners on second and third after Murcer circled in and trapped a sinking pop. With two outs, pinch hitter John Lowenstein lifted a fly to short center. Jones, who played a shallow centerfield early in the season, was now very deep; he raced in but pulled up short to play the ball on a bounce and two runs scored. Maybe he wouldn't have caught it if he had kept running and even dived. But there was nothing to gain by stopping. A Brett, Yastrzemski or Rose understands the situation and goes all out. That's the only way to make the play that separates a championship team from an also-ran.

If the Orioles can keep the pressure on, the Yankees have a week to acquire some tournament toughness. Otherwise, September will, after all, be very interesting.

Monday, August 11. Would you believe, we have a pennant race going! While I was off at the beach this weekend, the Orioles went to town and when the Yankees reached back to answer, there was nothing there. I came back to New York Sunday night and could scarcely believe what I heard on Sports Extra: the Birds *swept* the Yankees and trail New York by only 2½ games, a trifle of a margin at this point of the season.

The losses, moreover, were hard ones for the Yankees to swallow. The Orioles scored four runs in the eighth and ninth to win Friday, 5–2; two runs in the eighth to win Saturday, 4–2; and two runs in the ninth to win Sunday, 6–5. In their eighth and ninth innings, the Yankees got a total of nothing. Howser had carefully set up the pitching rotation for this series, but Guidry lost, John lost and Gossage allowed four runs to score in a total of two innings pitched. Worst of all, perhaps, was the outfield defense. Murcer, Jones, Jackson and Brown each failed to make catches that would have cut off Oriole rallies. Brown's miscue, in the ninth inning of the final game, was especially galling because he was in the game for defensive reasons.

Lapses in the Yankee outfield are not bad breaks. They are to be expected from a team that for several years has had the worst defensive outfield in the majors. They are the risk the Yankees are running by giving leftfield to an experienced bat and rightfield to Reggie. Jones and Brown may be adequate major league outfielders, though neither has shown much more than speed yet, but the other four on the squad are strictly DH-city. Which the Yankee brass has now admitted by quickly recalling my man Joe Lefebvre from Columbus.

Reggie went 1-for-8, without his 400th homer, but the Bird pitchers, like everyone else in recent weeks, were pitching around him. The spot behind Reggie in the batting order was a collective 0-for-11. Maybe it is too early to celebrate. But it is a good time for hope—the first time a Yankee-hater has had any in the last two months. And it is sure going to make a visit to Baltimore next weekend a lot more interesting.

Tuesday, August 12. In honor of the visiting delegates to the Democratic Convention, the *New York Times* polled "distinguished New Yorkers": "If a visitor were to ask your advice on the one thing to do here if he had only limited time, what would you suggest?" Messrs. Carey, Moynihan and Papp suggested the Metropolitan Museum, Central Park and the Empire State Building. Reggie Jackson suggested Jim McMullen's, a rather conventional Upper East Side restaurant that Reggie frequents after home games. Presumably the chance of seeing Reggie eating dinner is worth a couple of Michelin stars for any tourist.

Reggie also dropped McMullen's name in a *Sports Illustrated* cover story last month. And there was McMullen's in the paper again today. As Reggie left the restaurant and got into his Rolls-Royce late Monday night, after celebrating his 400th home run, a 16-year-old stuck a .45 in his ear and tried to steal the car. The youth eventually ran away, but Reggie admitted, "I was never so scared in my life." It was also probably just the right thing to convince the hordes from Alabama and Utah to steer clear of McMullen's—and visit Central Park instead.

Wednesday, August 13. Just when we are gearing up for a climactic five-game series with Baltimore and, out of the blue, a dramatic stretch run between two top baseball teams, the Yankees change the rules. How can anyone help but hate a team that, when the going gets tough, doesn't pull together to meet the challenge but instead runs out and buys another $200,000-a-year pitcher from Texas? The Yankees have a reputation for "buying" pennants, and if Gaylord Perry helps them to this one, the charge will be justified.

But they didn't buy, you say, they traded—and in any trade a team has to give as much as it gets. Apparently not, for all that Texas received in the deal was Ken Clay, whom Steinbrenner publicly labeled "gutless" last year, and was neither on the Yankee team this year nor in the Yankee plans for the future.

The Yankees aren't the only team that picks up late-season help for the pennant race—Kansas City tried to get

Sparky Lyle from Texas a couple of weeks ago—but it seems as if they do it more than anyone else. Or more than is necessary if you consider last year when the Yankee players pronounced their season over on July 29 but Steinbrenner nevertheless obtained Lenny Randle and George Scott in mid-August. Like most of these late-season pickups, they weren't around when the next season opened. But a fading veteran like Rodriguez or Perry will frequently rise from his rut and contribute a couple weeks of good play when given the challenge of proving himself to a new team in a pennant race. The new player may also have the effect—as ex-Met Randle was clearly intended to last summer, when Nettles, Dent and Stanley were all unsigned for 1980—of shaking up the complacency of the regulars, making them feel they have competition and reminding them that they could end up in even worse places than Texas.

The Yankees, I should add, also gave up a minor league "player to be named later." I have never figured out how that part of a deal works. Of course, in a deal with Texas it is probably some mythical figure, or inside joke, who keeps getting passed back and forth when one team unloads its rejects on the other.

Thursday, August 14. Meanwhile in the land of hype and money, the Los Angeles Dodgers are moving closer to another potential World Series showdown with the Yankees. And in a special treat that comes along only once every two weeks, NBC will carry the Dodgers-Reds game on TV next Saturday afternoon. But the same old pennant race is small avocados compared to the big news out of El Lay this week that Ken and Barbie, I mean Steve and Cyndy, Garvey have won a court order blocking the *Los Angeles Herald-Examiner* from reprinting a magazine article about their marital problems.

This is news to me first as a press lawyer, because until now American courts have said that the only kind of publication they can prohibit is something affecting national security. Granted, the Garveys may be national monuments—if I remember correctly, there is a junior high school in California that was named for Steve after the students' first choice, Elvis Presley, was turned down—but it is hard to figure how Cyndy's statement, "I'm a girl who needs a regular sex life," could endanger the republic, or even the TV talk show she cohosts in the mornings. The Garveys' lawsuit, based on the writer's supposed failure to keep a promise to write a "favorable" article, could put a lot of interviewers out of business if it succeeds, which, since the U.S. Constitution still applies to Los Angeles County, it won't.

The second significance of the news is that there is, in the words of the article's headline, "Trouble in Paradise." A small wave of pleasure laps over me whenever I read of a disturbance in the Dodgers' psyche, because since 1957 I have gone from loving the Dodgers to thinking of them as the Yankees of the West.

The first alienation of affection came with their treacherous flight to California in 1957. Not only did they desert faithful fans in Brooklyn (where I had never been), they took the Giants with them, emptying out the Polo Grounds I used to visit with my National League-loving father. Two teams were gone from my immediate universe—from the daily papers, the weekend TV and, not counting Les Keiter's play-by-play re-creations, the bedside radio. In their place was a disillusionment I have had to fight ever since: the realization that baseball is a business, and that the people who run it are influenced by a desire to make money. (The Fifties, as they say, was a simpler time.)

Then in the Sixties, California began to threaten New York, and the East in general, as the place where the action —cultural, political, social, athletic and pseudoreligious—was, and the Dodgers were clearly *the* team of these forces. In the Seventies there was a new reason to be turned off by the Dodgers, and his name was Tommy Lasorda. If it was hard to stomach Billy Martin's worshipful attitude toward the Yan-

kee pinstripes, it was worse to read Lasorda, who in his prime
was an even more trivial player than Martin, say that when
he cut himself he bled Dodger blue. I mean, the guy was
serious. If for Lasorda the Dodgers were a mission, for the
rest of us they were showbiz, and part of the whole Southern
California lifestyle.

The climax to my disaffection came in the 1978 World
Series when Lasorda's supposed Sunshine Boys squared off
for a rematch with the openly feuding Yankees. I had rooted
for the Dodgers, on Yankee-hating principle, in the 1977
Series and accorded Reggie only a grudging respect for his
three-homer performance mainly because of its perfection:
each homer was on the first swing and came off a different
pitcher, the last a knuckleballer. The '78 series started off
famously, with rookie Bob Welch striking out Reggie in a
classic *mano-a-mano* which Reggie polluted the next day by
complaining he had been distracted by his own teammate
breaking from first on the 3–2 pitch. Then I was livid when
Reggie won the pivotal fourth game by sticking his hip in the
way of a potential inning-ending doubleplay throw to first,
enabling the tying run to score. It was not just that Reggie
should have been called for interference but wasn't; it was that
no other player would have pulled such a stunt in the first
place. Instead of leading the Series, the Dodgers were tied
2–2, and with huge leaks sprouting in their infield defense
they were sinking fast.

And then they blamed their collapse on New York City
and the weirdos that live here! This was how they honored
their heritage, including Junior Gilliam, to whose memory they
were allegedly dedicating this Series. "You've got to be half-
crazy to live in this town," said shortstop Bill Russell after
his third error. "The fans are no good, just like the infield,
just like the writers, just like the weather." Second baseman
Davey Lopes, on the Yankees' comeback: "Maybe the city's
got something to do with it. You get rats cornered and they
fight back." And from outfielder Reggie Smith, the diplomatic

approach: "We're spending all our money to try to solve the problems in the Middle East. We ought to be spending it on educating these idiots here."

That's where I get off, fellas. I'll take bag ladies in the street and graffiti on the subways over mellowed-out surfers in hot tubs any day. When it was clear that this Dodger team just didn't have it, and when Jim "Catfish" Hunter, who had been a class act through the turmoil around him all year, went out to pitch the sixth (and final) game, I found myself actually rooting for the Yankees for the first time in my life.

Maybe it's none of the public's business to know that Cyndy Garvey thinks her husband egotistical, emotionally immature and, for her needs, sexually inadequate. It was, nevertheless, the best article about a ballplayer's private life—and the difference between being a baseball star and being a human being—that I have ever read. And when I read about a silly lawsuit in that sunny, wholesome, short-haired Dodger-blue paradise, I have to admit that, even as a Yankee-hater, I love it.

Friday, August 15. The Yankees are panicking! They managed two measly hits off Baltimore's Steve Stone who, according to the Yankee announcers, didn't have his good stuff all night. And instead of shaking it off as a mid-August slump, voices are pointing to Watson, Cerone, Jones and Soderholm—the newcomers who haven't been through a pennant race before —and insinuating, if they're like this the first time the Orioles make a run, what will they be like in September?

Of course, some of these voices are not totally objective: Piniella and Murcer, nothing if they are not veterans, are battling for playing time and would personally profit from a go-with-the-vets policy. And Reggie has managed to use the issue to, once again, call attention to himself. After homering off Stone for New York's only run in Thursday's 6–1 loss, Jackson stated his preference to be surrounded by people who have been through it before, instead of guys "on trial." Then today he noted that he has wanted to call a team meeting for a week, "but I couldn't do it 'cause I was playing well and I felt some of the guys who were struggling wouldn't take it right." Right, Reggie, it's better just to discuss it with the press.

Saturday, August 16. Baltimoreans this week are ripping mad, and the immediate cause was on the mound in Memorial Stadium tonight. Gaylord Perry, you see, epitomizes the difference between the New York and Baltimore philosophies of baseball. This is not a subtle observation I am making. I came down to Baltimore for tonight's game, and in two days' worth of *Baltimore Suns* I have found four articles and two letters to the editor devoted to this exact point. Even at the ballpark, I was bombarded with the same message from one of the two individuals who kept parading in front of my seat. The other was Pat "Bugler" Walker, a lumpy (if not loony) self-designated number 66 who led "Charge" cheers with a five-and-dime flugelhorn. But the first was a sanely dressed man who carried a stenciled sign proclaiming Look What Money Can't Buy—Total Class. And presumably he was referring to the team on the field, not Bugler Pat.

The people of this city are obsessed on the subject of buying players, and after George Steinbrenner their second bêtest noire is the Orioles' new owner, Edward Bennett Williams. Since he bought the team last year, he has threatened to move the franchise to Washington, his hometown, if attendance didn't improve. But he struck an even rawer nerve this week when he argued that increased attendance was necessary if the Orioles were to remain competitive in the free-agent market. "Don't you understand, Mr. Owner," came the editorial cries this weekend, "that people around here *don't want* free agents; that the O's have the best record in the American League over the last twenty-three years *without* free agents; that when free agency started Baltimore lost Grich, Jackson, Garland, Grimsley, Maddox—and in 1979 they still won the pennant; that Earl Weaver and General Manager Hank Peters have built team after team from inside the organization and through smart trades. We prefer to match our brains and our hard work—scouting, teaching, developing and molding—against the Yankees' money, and if we don't win every time, we'll feel suitably deserving when we do. If you're going to chase after free agents and start paying ridiculous salaries to over-the-hill journeymen, then you might as well take 'your' Orioles to Washington.''

Interestingly, Baltimore does have one free agent and he happens to be the player most responsible for their being in the pennant race this year. His name is Steve Stone. But Baltimoreans excuse this foray into the marketplace by pointing out (1) that no one really thought Stone, with a lifetime mark of 67–72, was very good (the Orioles accepted his contract demand for a bonus should he win the Cy Young Award because they thought he was kidding) and (2) that they got him for a measly $200,000 a year, free-agent chickenfeed.

And whereas Stone can be excused as the exception that proves Baltimore's rule, Gaylord Perry is all too typical for New York. He came from outside the Yankee organization (814 games outside, in fact). He has, in recent years, bounced from team to team, looking for somebody who would pay the exorbitant salary he demands. (He has bounced so much that while he is the only pitcher to win 100 games and the Cy Young Award in each league, each of these four landmarks was achieved with a different team.) He is a star on an individual level, being famous not only for throwing a spitball but for writing a book about it. And he was acquired by the Yankees on August 13, an unfairly late date, just when the Orioles thought they had the Yankees' number, just as they were licking their beaks at the prospect of facing the now demoted rookie Mike Griffin.

The Oriole fans and I, unfortunately, had to swallow our contempt for Perry and the Yankees this time, as Gaylord held the Birds completely at bay for seven innings. The longest hit he allowed was a 410-foot drive to dead center by Eddie Murray leading off the second. When Ruppert Jones leaped over the fence to catch it—about the first time this season a Yankee outfielder has challenged a fence, let alone won—the tenor of the game was established in the visitors' favor. To the credit of the Baltimore fans, or maybe it was just the surprisingly large contingent of Yankee supporters present, Perry got a good hand when he left the game in the eighth. The Goose put down six in a row to cap the Yankees' 4–1 win, and the Orioles, after two straight losses, gave every appearance of being critically wounded by a rejuvenated Yankee lineup. By evening's end, the only Baltimorean I could describe as ripping mad was Earl Weaver, who in the top of the eighth put on an enraged-manager act that was totally uncalled for, was thoroughly enjoyed by the fans and will serve as a textbook of moves for protesting managers for years to come.

Sunday, August 17. You know you've got a pennant race going when the conductor on the Sunday evening Metroliner announces, as the train is approaching Wilmington, Delaware, "A baseball score: Baltimore one, the Yankees nothing." It looks like I buried the Orioles prematurely, and when I heard that news, I was very glad to admit it.

Monday, August 18. The climactic fifth game of the Oriole-Yankee series came in three parts. Part 1 was the first 3½ innings, in which Baltimore threatened each time at bat and didn't score, while the Yankees got a total of one walk and one hit, good for two runs. Part 2 was the next 1½ innings, in which Baltimore scored six times, with the help of two surprise hits by Mark Belanger and some inadequate Yankee defense. Part 3 was the final 3½ innings, when I was having my anniversary dinner with my wife, praying that Palmer would hold the 6–2 lead. He didn't, as the Yankees scored three in the eighth, but a well-rested Tim Stoddard struck out the toothless Bucky Dent looking with men on second and third in the ninth to preserve a 6–5 win.

If it was the greatest series of the year, I missed something. The biggest game of all—Friday night when the Yankees had lost four in a row to the Orioles and had to win—and today's series finale—to determine whether the Yankees took a 2½-game or a 4½-game lead to the West Coast—were not televised in New York. Channel 11 claimed that today's unusual 5 o'clock game time would interfere with its newscasts. At the same time, Baltimore's mayor, a more astute politician, was making news by letting all city employees leave work early to watch the game against "the hated Yankees." Although three of the games wound up with close final scores, a lead changed hands only once in the five days, and that came in the fourth inning today. The Saturday night game in Baltimore was probably the least interesting game I have attended so far this year. And although it was the last meeting of the year between the only two contenders for the Eastern crown, the fact that the meeting came in mid-August, with 45 games left on each team's schedule, diminished the urgency considerably.

What did give the series landmark status was the attendance figures. For years to come I will be able to say that I was a part of the Orioles' second-largest regular-season crowd in history (after only "Thanks, Brooks" Night) and part of the largest one-series attendance total in baseball history. Since the baseball season contains very few five-day series, the record is something of a fraud. And since we broke the 17-year-old record by 34,688, it is hard for me to claim much credit.

Wednesday, August 20. Just when you thought it was safe to go back in the water, here comes George Steinbrenner, jawing away at the thrashing bodies on the Yankees. On Eric Soderholm: "He's been ridiculously bad; he's killed us." On Jim

Spencer: "A disappointment all year." On Bob Watson: "Sixty-seven percent of the times we have failed to deliver it has been the fifth hitter who has failed." On Reggie Jackson: "Reggie hit .120 in the Baltimore series. If that isn't tanking, I've never seen tanking." On Dick Howser: "Our guy is a freshman manager and he made some mistakes." Rick Cerone was also criticized, and Ron Guidry is to be given remedial pitching lessons.

George was in Tampa, meeting with the Yankee "brain trust," when he made these and other observations on the five-game Baltimore series. The objects of his derision were in Seattle. The press performed the painful but necessary chore of delivering the messages, and then was not above waiting around for the responses, which ranged from Soderholm's revelation that his wife has been in the hospital the last two weeks with a uterine infection to Jackson's *Roots*-like put-down: "It's like my father always told me. When the man don't know, the man don't know and don't pay no attention to him."

Everybody knows that the Yankees have not been hitting, and Steinbrenner's efforts to shake things up probably can't hurt matters too much. Spencer, Watson and Soderholm hardly represent the Yankees' investment in the future anyway. More problematic is the boss's attack on the manager and his staff, the people whose instructions the players are supposed to be following. They are helped somewhat, however, by the fact that everyone agrees that on the one "mistake" Steinbrenner cited, he doesn't know what he is talking about.

The issue is how Howser should have played the ninth inning of Monday's game after Bob Watson(!) led off with a pinch-hit(!) single. The Yankees were losing 6–5 and had Soderholm, Cerone, Jones, Dent and Stanley—all but Jones righthanded hitters—due up against flame-throwing righty reliever Tim Stoddard. On the bench was lefty Joe Lefebvre plus one reserve infielder should the game go to the bottom of the ninth. It turned out that Soderholm fanned, Cerone hit a fly, Jones singled and stole second and Dent took a 3–2 slider on the outside corner, leaving runners at second and third, Chicken on deck and Steinbrenner apoplectic. The *Post* found players who thought Howser should have pinch-hit Lefebvre for Soderholm. The *Times* suggested that Lefebvre should have pinch-hit for Dent. Howser said he was saving Lefebvre to pinch-hit for Stanley—not unreasonable in view of the walk Dent almost got and the potential embarrassment of having to let Stanley squawk for himself with the bases loaded and two out in the ninth. George, with excellent hindsight, would have opted for a fourth course: he would have had Soderholm bunt the runner over to second, whence he would have scored on Jones's single. "I don't believe that horseshit that you don't play for a tie on the road," said the owner with finality.

As for those of us who remember the hard time Steinbrenner gave Murcer when Bobby second-guessed the manager, George pointed out the difference in the two situations: "I'm the owner and I pay the bills."

Thursday, August 21. Remember Seattle? In the aftermath of the Oriole series, the exchange of insults between Steinbrenner and his employees, and the excitement of George Brett's remarkable assault on a .400 season batting average, the Yankees' final appearance of the season in Seattle has gone all but unnoticed. None of the three late-night games is being televised back to New York, and unlike the case with Monday's game in Baltimore, no one is complaining. The last two nights I have listened halfheartedly to the first few innings, until Bob Watson hits a home run, and I leave the inevitable news of another Yankee victory to the morning, hoping only that the Orioles have had similar success against California.

Even with new manager Maury Wills at the helm (a baseball cliché that for once seems appropriate), the Mariner games with New York seem to be played at a lower level of intensity than Yankee games anywhere else in the league. Is

Seattle that rarity of rarities, a town without Yankee-haters? I found an answer and saved a bunch from my research budget when my best friend from elementary-school days came through New York last week on vacation from his law practice in Seattle.

"People in Seattle don't hate anybody," Larry explained succinctly. "They are fanatic sports fans, though the Mariners are starting to test that fanaticism. But their rooting is all pro-Seattle, not against anybody. There's a let's-pull-together-for-the-Pacific-Northwest mentality in everything. When Darrell Johnson was the manager, everyone knew he was terrible, but nobody blamed him or made him a scapegoat.

"Of course, Seattle fans like to beat the Yankees most, but that's largely because they are the best, they represent excellence. Seattle would never operate the way the Yankees do, either. The idea of signing expensive free agents is repulsive. None of the Seattle teams is individual-oriented. If someone gets too big or wants too much money, the Seattle fans are glad to get rid of him. They wouldn't want a manager who was the whole show, like Martin or Williams or Weaver. When the [football] Seahawks had the first draft choice, they could have gotten Tony Dorsett, but they preferred to trade it to Dallas for three or four lower-level team players. Jim Zorn and Steve Largent are typical Seattle heroes—they're not big names, they don't make big money, and they regularly go to church. Seattle also likes to grow its own. Ruppert Jones was the Mariners' first star—and then, of course, he went off to the Yankees. How good was he in Seattle? Well, let's just say he was a lot better than Jim Beattie."

There is one other factor my friend didn't mention, perhaps because his judgmental powers have been Seattled. The Mariners this year have far and away the worst team and the worst record in the major leagues. When your team is that bad, you can't be too disappointed when they lose to anybody, let alone the Yankees.

Friday, August 22. Have you ever seen grown men panic? I give you the last twenty-four hours in the life of the New York Yankees and will let you watch for yourself.

Ron Guidry, recently considered the best pitcher in the American League, volunteered to become a relief pitcher and Howser agreed, at least until "he gets back to what he was."

Bobby Murcer, the number four lefthanded-hitting outfielder on the team, will start working out at first base, to replace Jim Spencer. This is Steinbrenner's brainstorm. Spencer's reaction: "I hope he can learn in a week what it took me 26 years to learn."

Until he does, Spencer is starting against righthanders, including Seattle's tonight. Ten days ago Bob Watson was installed as the full-time first baseman, but after Watson went 0-for-6 against the first two righties he faced, he was quietly disinstalled.

Brian Doyle, the human yo-yo, was sent down to the minors ten days ago and brought back up today.

Joe Lefebvre, who was brought up from Columbus ten days ago to be the leftfielder against righty pitching, played two games in left without a hit. Oscar Gamble has been there since.

Murcer and Piniella, the aged lefty-righty duo who have split everything so far this season—leftfield, DH and bitching to the press—started the same game last night. Against Seattle's lefthanded pitching, the righty got four hits, the lefty none.

The Yankees gave the punchless Mariners four first-inning runs on one hit. There were two errors by Aurelio Rodriguez filling in at second base, a stolen base when no one covered second, a wild pitch, two throws to the wrong base and two walks.

The Yankees got those four runs back, then lost 6–4. They left fourteen men on base, including three in the ninth.

Eric Soderholm struck out in the ninth with the bases

loaded and no outs. "It's funny," he commented. "I used to be a pretty good clutch hitter."

The Orioles beat the California Angels 7–1, sweeping that series, giving them a 5-game winning streak and cutting the Yankee lead to 1½ games.

"There are too many goddamn games left," said Piniella, "and we're playing each game like we've *got* to win. You start playing like that and you get burned out in two weeks." Added Reggie, lapsing into third-personese, "We've got too far to go. The Big Man has to stay cool. He can't be panicking."

A Yankee coach, anonymous, attacked Steinbrenner: "George is just putting too much pressure on them." George explained his "calculated" criticisms: "I felt the players needed something to get mad about. I don't want them to love me. I just want them to win."

It is not a pretty sight.

Chapter 8
WATCHING THE SEASONS CHANGE
And Other Media Matters

Saturday, August 23. The last five days there has been no Yankee baseball on television. Instead, Channel 11 has treated us to daily doses of "The Three Stooges," "The Odd Couple," "Twilight Zone Hour," and "Prisoner: Cell Block H." As a result, I have been unable to watch the saga of The Incredible Shrinking Lead, which during this period has dwindled from 3½ games to that smallest of baseball fractions, one half game.

This afternoon, the pennant race reappeared on the tube twice over: while Channel 11 was bringing us the Yankee game against the Angels, NBC's backup crew was in Oakland with the Orioles. Both Eastern teams won, and Rudy May looked just as sharp winning his 11th game as Steve Stone did winning his 21st. But while the Yankee defense—this time Jones and Watson—continued to let in runs, Baltimore's came up with the play of the day.

Second-string catcher Dan Graham's home run gave Baltimore a 3–0 lead until the seventh, when Oakland rallied for a run and Weaver replaced Stone with the sometimes erratic Tippy Martinez, who proceeded to wild pitch a second run home. Then he walked the bases loaded and went to a 3–2 count on Oakland outfielder Dwayne Murphy. With two outs, the bases loaded and the count full, everyone would be in motion. Martinez stretched . . . and threw to first! First baseman Eddie Murray, on a timed play, had sneaked in behind the runner and made an easy tag on Rickey Henderson to end the inning. What a beautifully conceived and executed play, and what a perfect time to use it. The aggressive baserunning that Billy Martin brags about was adroitly turned against him; the 21-year-old Henderson, who is very fast but not very savvy, was a sitting duck.

When was the last time the Yankees pulled such a gem? Martin, who has won several games this year for Oakland with improbable steals of home, has said he couldn't use such plays when he was at New York. Despite the annual efforts of Phil Rizzuto in spring training, it is questionable whether more than two or three Yankees know how to bunt, and the Yankees have to rank pretty low in such statistics as sacrifices and stolen bases. Yankee supporters may dismiss this as a matter of style: with all the home-run hitters the Yankees have, why risk anything with the small stuff? But the small stuff is fun, the small stuff is exciting, and the small stuff just may give you an edge when your home-run hitters aren't producing.

Moreover, the small stuff is what *team* baseball is all about. To make it work, the star must let himself be drilled in subtle maneuvers, not just fielding grounders and swinging for the fences. And he must be alive to every situation in the game. Home-run hitter Eddie Murray had to see the pickoff sign—from Weaver? Martinez? the rookie Graham?—and probably acknowledge it, too, so there was no chance of a run-scoring balk. While all other thoughts in the stadium and in the TV audience were trained on the climactic 3–2 pitch and the individual confrontation of pitcher and batter, some minds were whirring on a different level. And of the two teams fighting for the lead in the American League East, only Baltimore plays that kind of baseball.

Monday, August 25. The Yankees and the Orioles both lost to-night, only the second time in the last thirty days that has happened, and this has slowed the pennant race just enough for us to catch our breath and look at what lies ahead. The Yankees have 38 games left, slightly less than one-quarter of the season, and they are dead even with Baltimore, not counting the one extra game the Yankees have played and won. The two teams' schedules for the remainder of the season are virtually identical: both teams will host visits by the three West Coast power failures, then will spend the final month playing home-and-away series against four teams—Detroit, Cleveland, Toronto and Boston. In Steinbrenner's recent address to the troops he claimed, "I've studied the schedule for four or five days, and we will prevail." In the circumstances, the only thing more preposterous than saying that scheduling differences will be a significant factor in the stretch is claiming to have studied the schedule "for four or five days."

Who do I think will prevail? I picked the Orioles to beat the Yankees before the season started and I am sticking with them. (Actually, I picked Milwaukee to win and Baltimore to come in second; at the same time, I picked the Texas Rangers to win in the West, and they are now 19½ games out.) The key is pitching. In Stone (21–4), McGregor (15–6), Flanagan (13–9) and Palmer (13–9), Baltimore has the best pitching rotation in the majors, while the Yankees' rotation has been reduced to a patchwork. New York's supposed ace, Tommy John, is 2–4 with a 7.65 ERA for the last month. Guidry is being wasted in the bullpen, Perry is a .500 pitcher over the last two years and Tiant has pitched well but has lost his last five outings. May and Underwood shuttle to and from the bullpen. Whom would you put on the mound if the season were on the line? I don't think Howser knows the answer. The two teams' hitting is about the same, but with Nettles and Randolph out, the Orioles have an edge in the field.

The Yankees tonight lost Ruppert Jones for the season, but I am not sure which team that helps. I am sorry for his sake that he was hurt, and I always prefer to see the Yankees lose when the whole team is healthy. But sympathy aside, Jones was hitting a feeble .223 and had, with the exception of two fine catches at Baltimore, failed to distinguish himself in a Yankee outfield that is nothing if not undistinguished. Nor had he given any indication that he was ready to handle his first pennant race with the New York media and a fanatic owner breathing down his neck. After the second Baltimore series he told the press: "You guys write whatever you want. I've just had it. It's been a tough year all around."

The other thing to remember is that while his replacement, Bobby Brown, has a glove that is more brass than gold, his brassiness helps him on the basepaths, he is a switch-hitter with a 40-point-higher average than Jones, and he has hit just as many home runs (9). Moreover, the Yankees' best streak of the year (26–12) came when Jones was on the disabled list the first time.

Tuesday, August 26. Credit Billy Martin with the game-winning run-batted-in in Oakland's 3–1 win over the Yankees tonight. This is a new and relatively undiscovered statistic, being kept officially in the American League for the first time this year. I happen to know all about it because three months ago I wrote to Question Box, a regular feature in the *New York Times*'s SportsMonday section, and a month later they published my question and the answer. More amazing, four days after I mailed my letter, I got a lengthy personal reply from the *Times*'s assistant sports editor, giving me a sneak preview as well as answers to two other questions I had asked, intending to increase my chances of getting published.

My first question asked who chooses Gold Glove winners, which is an award I never heard of as I was growing up but which is the accepted measure of defensive excellence today. It turned out that this had been covered "in a previous column" (which the editor thoughtfully enclosed). My second question was how many times has the "save" rule for relief pitchers been changed. This, too, was not a part of remembered child-hood catechism, and furthermore I had detected a noticeable devaluation of the requirements in recent years. This had been discussed "on two different times, at least, in the column," but I was given the courtesy of a third answer as well as a photocopy of the current rule.

I hit the jackpot, however, with my question on the game-winning RBI, although I had mistakenly referred to it as "game-winning hit." It was published as the third question, out of ten, in the column for June 23, the leadoff spot going to the illustrated question—"Can a switch-hitter change sides during a time at bat?"—with a nonbaseball query tossed in second for variety—"Did Sid Terris ever win the lightweight title?" (If you think that's obscure, how about this one from yesterday, probably propounded by the same 70-year-old boxing nut: "How old was Battling Siki, who won and lost the light heavyweight title, when he was murdered in New York City?")

The first part of my question was easily fielded: the "GWRBI" was making its AL debut a year after Mike Schmidt won the National League's first crown with 20 in 1979. The second part—what determines a GWRBI—had a deceptively simple answer, but therein lay a problem. It is the RBI "that gives a club a lead it never relinquishes." Period. Nothing else matters, including the inning in which this event occurs. Which casts some shadow on the significance of this statistic. Obviously, if the score is tied 3–3 in the ninth and Reggie drives in a run for a 4–3 win, that RBI deserves to be recorded as a measure of clutch performance. But let's take a more prosaic example, from last Wednesday's 6–4 win over Seattle. The Yankees scored one run in the second, but the Mariners got two in the bottom of the inning. The Yankees answered with two more in the third, the second on a Jackson single, for a 3–2 lead. The Yankees went up 6–2 with three in the seventh, and the Mariners scored two in the ninth, to make the final score 6–4. The GWRBI did not come on the fifth run, driven in by Murcer's double in the seventh; it was Reggie's less-than-momentous ribbie back in the third.

There was one person on whom the significance of that hit was not lost, however. On the radio the next night Phil Rizzuto asked Bill White how one got a GWRBI and White guessed wrong. According to the Scooter: "I asked everybody in the clubhouse today, the sportswriters, everybody, and the only person who knew the rule was Reggie. And I knew it was right when Reggie told me, because he checks on those things." White, flabbergasted at Rizzuto's explanation, reduced the rule ad absurdum: "So if a guy puts his team ahead 1–0 in the first inning and the team never loses the lead, he gets the game-winning RBI even if the final score is 20–19!?" Rizzuto's final comment on the subject was to paraphrase a popular country-and-western song: "They should take that stat and shove it."

Reggie, I learned in the paper two days later, was not coincidentally leading the American League at the time with 13 GWRBIs, although since then I have read of several *real* game-winning hits by Al Oliver and George Brett, his closest competitors.

Billy Martin, strictly speaking, isn't in the competition, because companion rule 10.04 does not recognize RBIs by managers. But his contribution to last night's Oakland win was as valid and crucial as many of Reggie's 13. The Yankees got a run off Rick Langford in the first, and Luis Tiant retired the first thirteen batters in a row before Oakland's Tony Armas singled and scored on Mitchell Page's triple. Now everyone is approximately aware that Martin has successfully worked 13 suicide squeeze plays (in 19 attempts) with Oakland this year, and the Yankees felt the pressure when Page came charging home and Jim Essian squared to bunt. The bunt went foul but the shaken Tiant proceeded to walk Essian. A runner on first only increases Martin's options for trickery. Realizing this, the Yankees pitched-out, batter Mario Guerrero missed his bunt attempt, and Cerone had Page caught off third. With the retreating Page blocking his line of vision, however, Soderholm missed Cerone's throw and Page turned around and scored what proved to be the winning run. In all, the A's got three runs on only four hits off Tiant and Gossage, but Billy Martin's aggressive managing was, last night at least, the game-winning difference.

Thursday, August 28. I had lunch today with a former office-mate who has invited me to the Oakland game next Tuesday. He used pull to get his company box seats, and I am doing the same for a Cleveland game later in the month. Company boxes, I used to think, were something to be used by middle-aged men in suits, who never swore at the umpires and who left after the eighth inning to avoid the traffic jams. The true baseball fan like me, I believed, sat in the upper deck, preferably in section 1 right behind home plate. That seat gave me a better perspective on fly balls and on both foul lines than one could get downstairs, I was close to the action because of the upper deck's overhang, and I was free to move around if somebody near me had a radio. Best of all, the upper level general admission ticket, which gave one de facto sliding privileges down into the upper level reserve section, cost only $1.50.

In the last five years this bargain, the best in all of sports, has unfortunately disappeared. As the Yankees began to win with their free-agent stars, the stands began to fill up and the ticket prices went in the same direction. People even bought tickets in the upper level reserve section, which meant that that area was soon closed to sliding. The general admission section itself was moved further from the field, it was reduced in size and it became more crowded. In compensation, the price of the ticket went up to $2.75. And not only has the increased attendance wiped out the general admission seat as a serious option, it has meant that you can't count on getting good tickets at the gate even if you buy box seats for $7.50.

So I am preparing myself for the stretch run, during

which only 4 of the final 16 games are scheduled to be televised, by lining up corporate season ticket holders, telling
myself that I have not sold out and that I will yell my head off
unabashedly as before, even without upper-deck anonymity.

My friend, by the way, claims to be only a middling baseball fan, which was certainly more than enough to recognize
Reggie Jackson when he sat down in front of Bob on his flight
to Minneapolis last summer. Bob, following company policy,
was in the first-class section only because the coach section
was sold out. Reggie was there (without his team) because
he was either going to or coming from treatment for one of
his overmuscled-leg injuries. Reggie moved, however, as soon
as another first-class passenger sat next to him, and when the
adjoining seat at his new location was occupied, Reggie got
up, told the stewardess he wanted to look for two empty seats
together, and disappeared back in the coach section. As already
mentioned, however, the flight was sold out, and Reggie's
chances of finding peace and quiet in the common-people's
section were none and noner, and he was quickly back. The
day was saved when just before takeoff Harry Belafonte
boarded the plane; Reggie arranged to sit across the aisle
from his fellow superstar, and the two rapped contentedly all
the way to Minnesota.

The only disturbance was the constant stream of autograph seekers from coach who had learned of the Great Man's
presence on board when, in a typical Reggie irony, he went
looking for a quiet place to sit.

Saturday, August 30. The only chance the hopeless Seattle Mariners had tonight was for the league president to uphold Maury
Wills's protest against Gaylord Perry's red glove. Where Perry
would get a red glove I don't know, but I suspect that he was
using it tonight just the way he uses his spitball reputation.
The Mariners' problems, however, were not nearly so sophisticated. Centerfielder Juan Beniquez dropped two fly balls, let
Piniella tag and go to third on a routine fly that he did catch

and was out at home when Murcer decoyed him into thinking that Jerry Narron's drive to left was a ground-rule double. Danny Meyer made three bad plays at third base and Larry Milbourne was so worried about a runner at third that he let Jim Spencer slide safely under him at second without bending down to tag him. The Yankees' lead grew to 8–2 in the fifth when with two outs Brian Doyle struck out—and the pitch bounced past the catcher. Just when the announcers thought they had seen everything (another radio-only night), catcher Narron lost a pitch in his chest protector and Spencer took another base.

Rizzuto stuck up for fellow ex-shortstop Wills by saying he was trying to teach fundamentals to his new team every day before the game, and "Boy, they need it!" White pointed out the potential dangers of a late-season instructional blitz when you're dealing with players who think they are already major-leaguers. No one mentioned the possible futility of this approach when your starting lineup, however unfamiliar the names may be, has only one player under 27.

The best time, if not the only time, to teach fundamentals is when players are young, a point that was continually made earlier in the day by announcers Don Drysdale and Willie Stargell during the telecast of the Little League World Series final between teams from Taiwan and Tampa, Florida. No manager in America, it is safe to say, drills his team as thoroughly or as successfully as the Taiwanese. What is less obvious, however, is how the Chinese, whom we think of as relatively short people, can year after year produce Little League pitchers who are from six to seventeen inches taller than the American batters they have to face.

Watching this game, which Taiwan won as usual, prompted one observation, solved one mystery and raised another. The observation is that baseball *can* be a fast game. Every time the pitcher got the ball he threw it; every time someone went somewhere he ran—even to the dugout after striking out. No one argued, no one knocked the dirt out of his spikes, no one conferred at length on the mound, and because there is no leading before the pitch, the pitcher never checked the runner. This speedup did not, by any means, constitute an improvement; it did, however, keep the tension consistently higher throughout the game. The mystery solved is why so few of these phenomenally successful 12-year-old pitchers make it to the big leagues (remember Joey Jay?). If much of their success is due to early maturation, that will be no help once they are 23 and everyone else is just as big, if not bigger. In that sense, Little League is unfair in arbitrarily relying on birth dates. There is probably no other realistic line that can be drawn, but how many of us were scarred for life by the pitcher from the next town who seemed to be a different species, let alone a different age. He struck everyone out when he was 12, was picked up by the cops at 14 and seemingly disappeared from the face of the earth after high school.

The mystery that arose from watching the Florida kids play baseball not nearly as well as I do now is, why wasn't I a star in Little League, let alone in the Little League World Series? Sure, they're only 12, but I couldn't have gotten that much better in the last 22 years. Heck, some of those years I didn't even play ball.

Sunday, August 31. Amid the concern over how Soderholm and the other first-year Yankees are responding to their first pennant race, few have noticed that the person showing the greatest signs of stress since Baltimore started its run is a veteran of 23 Yankee pennant races, Phil Rizzuto. Today the Scooter was careening out of control in the radio and TV booth, even though the game at hand with Seattle was hardly a make-or-break affair. Baltimore, with Weaver serving a three-game suspension for his showboat routine against the Yankees two weeks ago, had just lost two straight to California, and New York had won three in a row from the Mariners, restoring a 2½-game lead.

"Every game from here on in is important," bubbled the

Scooter. "It's like the World Series, the tension in the air. I can't imagine how anybody would miss one of these games. I'm not gonna miss any more, that's for sure." "Wanna bet?" offered colleague Bill White, in a jibe at Rizzuto's Johnny Carson-like contract and his custom of listening to the final innings of radio broadcasts on the New Jersey side of the George Washington Bridge.

While getting out of work whenever he can is something that millions of his listeners can identify with, it is Rizzuto's openness in admitting this, or in saying anything else that comes to mind, that is his most endearing quality. "That's a lot of garbage," he responded today to a comment by Fran Healy, and when anybody gives him a hard time, Rizzuto will name-call back, "That huckleberry!"—and you just know that these aren't euphemisms, these are the strongest epithets in the Scooter's vocabulary.

Speaking of euphemisms and vocabulary, Rizzuto has a way with words that doesn't quite rise to the level of mala-propism, but isn't the right way, either. Seeing a fan's sign that proclaimed Piniella The Real Italian Stallion, Rizzuto pointed out that "Lou's descendants are actually from Spain." Piniella and Murcer are valuable players down the stretch be-cause of their "veteran wiseness." Today's game was delayed at the top of the eighth inning because "a couple of mullions" ran out to give Bucky Dent a hug. The inning before, Dent made a good play "on the second-base side of shortstop." Bits of folk wisdom, like today's sudden shower, come out of the blue: "They say rain makes you grow." After a Rodriguez error, he began to moralize, "Now there's a point in case." And Phil today changed his tune on Maury Wills's late-season instruction, saying he should save it for next spring: "The seed is planted in spring training, then nine months later frui-tion pays off. . . . Emily Dickinson is the one who told me about that."

At the age of 62, Rizzuto retains a kidlike enthusiasm for the game. When he saw that Wills lets a different Mariner take out the lineup card before each game, Phil said, "I would have liked to do that, and see what all the talk is that they have at home plate." If he were a manager, "I'd teach 'em trick plays. Oh, I'd have the fans screaming and jumping out of the upper deck." And when it comes to announcing the game, the listener has to wade through Phil's emotional outbursts to find out what is going on: "Holy cow! They'll never get Brown! What a beautiful bunt!"

Rizzuto's innocence is also a perfect conduit for Reggie's publicity mill. Friday night we heard that Reggie gave a glove to Fran to give to Phil to give to Scooter, Jr., down in South Carolina—and how thrilled Phil's son was going to be. ("If I were him, I'd sell it," cracked Healy.) Today we found out from Phil that Reggie was not scheduled to start, but when he saw the lineup card he jumped up from the trainer's table (where he was presumably near death) and insisted on playing. Why? "Because he realizes he has a shot at the MVP Award and he knows you don't win the MVP sitting on the bench." Reggie apparently neglected to remind Phil that you don't win the MVP Award either when George Brett is hitting .406, is tied or ahead of you in every offensive statistic except home runs, is a better fielder and baserunner and is playing on a team winning its division by 20 games.

When the excitement becomes too great—"The tension is unbelievable"—or the conditions unbearable—"It's very hot today and I'm a little light-headed"—Phil calms his nerves by reading birthday, anniversary and get-well greetings to the "paisans"—anyone with an Italian name. Today we heard that "Al and Rose Luzzi of Bayonne, New Jersey, had a baby girl," while "T. J. DeMarsica, a friend of Carmen Berra's, is in the hospital after a hit-and-run accident."

The only thing that calmed down the Scooter was the ninth inning when the Mariners scored the game's only run off reliever Guidry on a Baltimore chop that Randolph tried to short-hop but couldn't. When, in the bottom of the ninth, Dent, Rodriguez and Brown went down one-two-three, Rizzuto had no more big words, no more dedications, no more plugs for Jackson, and like a kid who has lost the big game, he was very subdued indeed.

Wednesday, September 3. In the entire three-game series just concluded with the Oakland A's, there was only one dramatic moment, and I was there. It came last night, during the second game, and it came without warning. Sitting in the front row of the loge section, behind the visitors' dugout, I had a perfect view of the action. The Yankees had just taken a 1–0 lead in the bottom of the fourth on doubles by Jackson and Piniella; with two outs Piniella had moved to third where he stood as Bucky Dent came to bat against the A's Brian Kingman.

Then a swirling wind swept over the leftfield fence and headed for home plate like it was still looking for Dorothy. The skies opened and the rain fell—not straight down but angling out toward center and sweeping in toward the backstop and swirling in circles, a constantly shifting pattern of white caught in the illumination from the light towers. Bolts of lightning creased the black sky above, mocking the home-run displays of other ballparks, and thunder resounded through the echoing caverns of Yankee Stadium. The ground crew rose to the occasion and laid the tarpaulin in a minute, then watched in awe as the wind exposed the left side of the infield and blew the heavy metal rollers toward the Yankee dugout. In ten minutes the rightfield corner was a swamp. Eddie Layton piped away on the Hammond organ, but he was no match for the voice of nature, announcing the end of the summer sauna, bringing us the fall.

After fifteen minutes the excitement was over and I went out for a knish and a soda. When I returned, the Yankee fans had begun to reclaim the stands: three teenagers were staging a water fight in a puddle left in the upper deck's first row, and rainsoaked signs of the pennant race—Boston Sucks and Baltimore Blows—were being held up in the leftfield boxes. After forty minutes, shortly followed by a less interesting twenty-minute delay, the game resumed and the Yankees rolled to a methodical 6–1 win, the exact margin of their 5–0 win the day before and their 8–3 win tonight. Underwood pitched a four-hitter Monday, May a six-hitter Tuesday, and John a five-hitter Wednesday. The A's have lost seven in a row and, like the summer sun, are sinking slowly in the West. Critics have said that baseball is too slow, that watching it is as exciting as watching grass grow. That is ridiculous. But if the opposition hits like the Oakland A's, and if you change the comparison to the rain falling as it did last night, then you've got a contest.

Thursday, September 4. Tonight the Yankees begin a four-game series with the California Angels which, I am glad to say, represents the last we will see of the American League's West Coast teams until 1981. Frankly, my biggest disappointment so far this year is not that the Yankees are doing so well but that the level of competition has been so low. New York, Baltimore and Boston—a third team that has appeared on the fringes of the race thanks to a nine-game win streak—are rattling off win after win, and I'd like to think what clutch baseball the veterans are playing now that it is September. Over the last 15 games, the Yankees' record is 10–5, Baltimore's 11–4 and Boston's 12–3. But I know that in this period these three teams have played only Seattle, California and Oakland. I probably should not limit my complaint to the West Coast teams. The entire AL West has 68 fewer wins than the East, and the second-place Texas Rangers have a record that would be good enough for seventh place in the East, a full 3½ games behind sixth-place Cleveland.

Friday, September 5. The Yankees and Orioles kept pace with equally improbable gift wins from their California cousins. The Orioles were losing to Oakland 7–5 in the bottom of the ninth when Al Bumbry hit a potential game-ending double-play grounder that went through the second baseman's legs. A sacrifice fly, a Singleton double and Baltimore had its win.

As for the Yankees, they tried hard to lose but California just wouldn't let them. When Bobby Brown singled to lead off the seventh with New York down 5–2, Fregosi brought in Andy Hassler, who is famous for losing games no matter how well, or where, he pitches. Hassler got a good start in that direction by walking Randolph, then Dent hit a hard grounder right to third. Lansford to Grich to Carew won't win any poetry awards, and their round-the-horn effort was so leaden that Bucky Dent beat the throw to first. Hassler walked Watson on four pitches. After Reggie fanned, Piniella grounded again to Lansford, who bobbled the ball, ran halfway to first with it, then fired it in the dirt, past Carew and into the stands. Catcher Dave Skaggs contributed a passed ball and Watson scored the tying run. Recognizing a good thing when he saw one, Cerone also grounded to Lansford, who took his time before making a low throw that Carew dropped. For no discernible reason, however, Piniella went back to third instead of scoring on the play, so the game eventually went into extra innings. With one out in the tenth, two Angel outfielders performed a pas de deux and Cerone's fly fell for a triple. Then with two outs and the bases loaded, Randolph checked his swing and sent a slow roller to second that he would have beaten out even if Grich had caught the ball, which of course he didn't.

If I were a Yankee fan, I'd be embarrassed to win a game like this.

Sunday, September 7. Today climaxed a terrible week for the Yankee-hater. Last Sunday night the Yankees had a one-game lead in the loss column over the Orioles, a five-game lead over the Red Sox, and George Brett was hitting .403. Tonight the Orioles are four games back in the loss column, the Red Sox a remote nine, and Brett is hitting .396 and on the bench with an injured wrist. To top it off, at the afternoon party my wife and I went to, the socially retarded men I followed off to a back room were not watching the Yankees beat the Angels or the A's upsetting Steve Stone but had commandeered a TV set to watch the New York Giants open the pro football season against the St. Louis Cardinals.

When George Steinbrenner spent four or five days dissecting the teams' comparative schedules, he cited Oriole makeup games in Boston and Detroit and a nonexistent four-game series in California as games that would make the difference. Dick Howser's oblique comment on this analysis came a week later: "Anybody who's got it figured out is not in baseball." On the week's evidence, Howser is closer to the money. While the Yankees predictably swept four games from the Angels, the Red Sox inconceivably lost three of four to the worst team in baseball, the Mariners. And the Orioles, pitching past, present and future Cy Youngers Palmer, Flanagan and Stone, lost three of four to Oakland.

The Yankees have loped off into the stretch run with their hitting shoes on. They have averaged six runs a game in their seven-game winning streak and are all of a sudden getting run production from people like Bucky Dent, Oscar Gamble, Bobby Brown and Jim Spencer, people we haven't heard from in months. Spencer took advantage of his game-winning home run today to remind The Man that he was still around. "I don't understand why I hit a three-run homer," Spencer said. "I've been just awful . . . I've disappointed George, the fans, the manager and even the batboy."

Now don't get too cocky, Jim. As Howser will tell you, it's a strange game and anything can happen. And if things start going too well, Ruppert Jones might come back.

Monday, September 8. Of all the unfair advantages the Yankees have in life, the one I resent the most is Rich Gossage. I don't so much care that he is another Steinbrenner free agent—I've come to expect that. What bugs me is that he is not only unbeatable, he's unhittable. Others have played his role before him: Joe Page, Ryne Duren, Luis Arroyo and Sparky Lyle are four other ways the Yankees have spelled relief in the last thirty-five years. But I can accord Gossage the highest accolade I can bestow upon a pitcher: even in my wildest daydreams I would not want to bat against him.

He comes on and throws heat. He barely slows down between pitches. He ignores the batter as well as the baserunners. He just gets the ball and fires—fast, faster and invisible. The good batters in the league like Carew can occasionally punch a fastball to the opposite field. But there aren't many Carews. The rookies and the marginal players that fill the expansion-riddled American League don't have a prayer and they know it. It is no contest, and that is not the way sport is supposed to be.

For some reason Gossage tends toward ineffectiveness if the Yankees have a big lead or are losing. But Howser hasn't used him in that situation since early in the season. The Goose does only one thing now: he comes on in save situations and pockets the save. I read in the *Post* today—and once you get past the first six pages the *Post*'s information is not necessarily wrong—that Gossage has picked up 24 saves in his last 26 save opportunities. Of the other two, one was a win and one a loss. So when the opposition sees Gossage on the mound, they know they have a 96 percent chance of losing.

Gossage has a 2.03 ERA, more strikeouts than innings pitched and a 6–1 record to go with his saves. But those are mere statistics. Look at this weekend's games. Friday night Gossage retired six Angels in a row before the Yankees came up with a run in the tenth to give him the win. Saturday night the Angels were down by two when Carew led off the eighth against Guidry with a triple. The Goose came in and not only got three straight outs, he stranded Carew at third. In the ninth he struck out the side. Sunday the Angels were down 4–1, but when they brought the tying run to the plate in the ninth Howser called on the Goose for the last two outs, one a strikeout.

Tonight the Yankees gave a lead to the Blue Jays, who are well past their breeding season, when Rodriguez threw a sacrifice bunt into rightfield for two runs and Brian Doyle threw a doubleplay attempt into the dugout for a third. Down 4–3 in the ninth, Murcer, Gamble, Watson and Cerone combined to hit for the cycle to give the Yankees a 7–4 lead. Gossage was tired and Tommy John was going for his 20th win, so Howser stuck with his starter—until Toronto loaded the bases with two outs. Enter the Goose: three strikes and another save. He has now retired 22 batters in a row and picked up four saves and a win in his last five appearances.

When I see Toronto take a 4–3 lead into the ninth I think: if only they had a reliever like the Goose, I could relax. When the Yankees take a lead into the ninth, I know the game is as good as over.

Tuesday, September 9. Apparently because the actors' strike in Hollywood has crippled the new fall season of mindless TV shows, the networks are turning to prime-time entertainment starring real people who are not members of the Screen Actors Guild. For NBC on Thursday night this will result in the heavily advertised premiere of "Games People Play," featuring a "Union Tug-of-War" between members of the United Mine Workers and the United Steelworkers of America, a "Prison Obstacle Race" between women inmates and correctional officers, and a "Record Bus Jump," a man-bites-dog reversal in which a school bus will attempt to leap over twenty motorcycles. That kind of show is more or less expected. Slightly more surprising is tonight's NBC broadcast of an actual, real game people play—baseball—a Tuesday night Game of the Week between the Astros and Starsky and Hutch, I mean, the Dodgers.

Since the Yankee series with Toronto is confined to the radio, I used the evening to scout my potential World Series team on the tube while keeping one ear tuned to the Yankee game in the background. Following two games simultaneously is a not-too-difficult skill I learned back in the days when New York had three major league teams. I also learned a corollary: in order to avoid the unctuous Mel Allen, I would, while watching the Yankee game on TV, turn off the sound and rely on Red Barber's broadcast of the same game on the radio. Both these practices taught me that—whether it was Allen or Russ Hodges or Vin Scully didn't matter—radio and TV broadcasts are very distinct forms of communication. On TV the announcers let the picture tell the story. They give the batter's average, tell what he's done earlier in the game and describe the plays as they occur. But they aren't afraid of momentary silences, the pauses that are a part of baseball's rhythm. The radio announcer, on the other hand, has to keep constant contact with his listener, to assure him, like a blind person, that he isn't missing anything. "Kucks goes to the resin bag . . . peers in for the sign . . . he's into the windup . . . here's the pitch" was the repeated, albeit meaningless, refrain.

Tonight, with Frank Messer and Bill White coming in one ear and Joe Garagiola and Tony Kubek the other, it was obvious that this accepted distinction has been rejected by network baseball. Kubek and Garage spoke more than twice as much as the radio announcers. And when they had nothing to say, they talked even more. They talked incessantly—about the fans, the umpires, the weather, NBC's fall lineup, the pennant races in the other divisions, other games they had seen, the World Series. When nothing was happening NBC had a radar gun inset in the picture that let you see the speed not only of Joaquin Andujar's fastball (93 mph), but also of the catcher's return throw (56 mph), Andujar's toss home to exchange baseballs (40 mph) and the umpire's lob back to the mound (34 mph). When something did happen, Kubek analyzed it to exhaustion. First baseman Art Howe leaned over the dugout railing to catch a foul pop and Kubek was off: "He got a lot of help from his Houston teammates in the dugout and he also got a lot of help from the pitcher Andujar who came all the way over" (and watched the play from a respectful distance).

There were frequent updates from Philadelphia, where what truly seemed to be a pennant race was underway between the Phils and the Pirates, and every few innings we in New York got an Election Report on Holtzman's win and Javits's loss in the Senate primaries. But what exhausted me as much as the amount of verbiage was the urgency in Joe's and Tony's voices. Garagiola seems to live in an upper register and Kubek realizes he has to practically shriek to blend in. Maybe the former Yankee shortstop has yet to recover from Bill Virdon's pivotal grounder in the seventh game of the 1960 World Series that hit him in the Adam's apple. Whatever the cause, his breathless wonderment never flags.

The Astros won 5–4 to move within one game of the first-place Dodgers, and the game was exciting, I guess. At least the fans waving orange placards with a large "Datsun" written across the bottom seemed about as worked up as Western Division fans get. But the normal pitch of the telecast was so high that when the game came down to the ninth inning, the announcers had nowhere to go. NBC had been pulling out all stops for three and a half hours, desperately trying to keep everyone from changing the channel. This baseball game, so unlike a real baseball game, was busy, busy, busy. The rhythm of the summer game was destroyed, and in its place NBC had cleverly substituted the pacing normally associated with a female inmates' obstacle race, or an ever popular NBA basketball game.

Whether it was due to the telecast or just the teams involved, there was much less drama for me in Houston than in the unseen games in Toronto and Detroit. The Yankees lost, the Orioles won, the lead is down to 3, and the pendulum in the AL East is swinging back once more.

Wednesday, September 10. The official Yankee schedule they give out at the Stadium was wrong—tonight's game *was* on TV, and I took advantage of my last chance to watch the Yankees play in Toronto's Exhibition Stadium. If I hadn't recognized the Yankee faces, I would have thought I was watching two second-division teams playing out the schedule. Except for the home bullpen, there was not a soul along the rightfield line. The small crowd was so quiet you could hear people talking near the announcers' booth, not to mention the occasional exhortation a fan was yelling at Toronto pitcher Jim Clancy. The lights were so dim that the artificial turf looked gray on my set.

The quality of play was dim as well. The Blue Jays got three runs in the first, helped by Spencer, Underwood and Rodriguez muffs and two wild pitches. In the second Underwood showed why pitchers aren't allowed to field popups when he dropped a bunt popped right to him. And in the third the Blue Jays almost put the game away when they scored three runs after Bucky Dent booted a ground ball with two outs and nobody on. White and Messer marveled at the Yankees' lack of concentration. Healy tried unsuccessfully to get Rizzuto to explain that even he couldn't play with intensity for an entire season, but the Scooter did offer that that had been true for Yogi. At bat the New Yorkers continued their futility: Reggie struck out two more times and they left seven men on base in the first four innings.

In between innings the cameraman tracked down Yankee fans with I Love Reggie and University Buffalo Loves Yankees signs, and I was struck by the contrast between the old and the new in American League cities. The pre-expansion cities are rife with Yankee-haters, and it takes a certain amount of courage or foolhardiness to parade a pro-Yankees sign in Boston, Detroit, Chicago or Cleveland (if anyone is there). On the other hand, if you watch a game in Oakland, Seattle, California or Toronto, you won't hear any boos, except for Reggie, and you will see more signs for New York than the home team. Before baseball came to these cities, there was little emotional reason to hate the Yankees, who were America's Team long before the Dallas Cowboys were born. And until these cities join Kansas City in accumulating their own history of being screwed by the Yankees, the townsfolk will treat them like visiting celebrities instead of the loathsome competitors their longtime rivals know them to be.

In all, tonight was shaping up as a quiet September evening, a pleasant, relaxing contrast to the hullabaloo on NBC last night. Then my roof caved in. Leading off the seventh, with the Yankees down 6–2, Willie Randolph had an 0–2 count—and got a walk. Playing as if last place was at stake (it's not), Toronto gave up five runs on two walks, two wild pitches, a doubleplay throw past first and four Yankee singles. And to make sure the 7–6 lead held, Howser brought in the Goose, who finished a string of 27 consecutive outs—a perfect game in relief—before ending the game with another strikeout.

Thursday, September 11. Monday Night Football made its annual debut three nights ago, but since it wasn't replacing Monday Night Baseball this year I took no umbrage at its arrival. What I do find uncalled for, however, is this "special edition" of Monday Night—otherwise known as Thursday Night—that ABC is foisting upon the L.A. Rams, the Tampa Bay Bucs and, they hope, millions of us sports nuts tonight. They would have us forget that the Yankees are opening a four-game series in Fenway Park, their first true test of the stretch drive.

I used to be a pro football fan with the best of them. In the newspaper column I wrote in college, "The Sports Dope," I was even the first person to predict that the AFL champion would win the Super Bowl—and it was only through bad timing that I graduated a year before this actually happened. But in the '70s pro football became a bit too cocky about supplanting baseball as the national pastime. The NFL also shamelessly flooded the market. Not only did it expand the sports weekend to Monday night, it hit us on Sunday with "regional doubleheaders." And like every other sports league, it added teams, lengthened the schedule, and opened more doors into the playoffs. Where before every game counted, the first six games of the season came to mean next to nothing. By common consent one no longer had to watch every pro football game carried on TV to be considered a serious sports fan. And once I realized I couldn't watch it all, it became easier to watch less and less.

The decisive date in my disaffection was August 1974. That month I married a woman with many charms and many virtues, but being a fan of TV sports was not one of them. And on our honeymoon I read *North Dallas Forty,* by one-time Dallas Cowboy end Pete Gent, a work that provided the moral underpinnings for my turn from football back to the gentler sport of baseball. Gent's book added a dimension—an ugly, sordid dimension—to the pro football game that existed on TV. For example, every day the sports pages carry news of a football injury, how it will affect a team's chances, what it does to the betting line. But Gent's book made me think what it did to the player: how he hurt, in his body and mind; how he would be rushed back into action with the help of painkilling drugs; how his club would use him, then discard him on the trash heap when they thought he could no longer do the job. One constant message was what glory and what recognition could come to you through football, and how little it had to do with decent human values. The fans, from the gas station attendant to the millionaire owner, sucked up to the football stars, seeking a reflected glory, then turned on them when some rookie took their job. And who cares what kind of person some defensive tackle is; the meaner he is the better, right? If he knocks the opposing quarterback out of the game, well those are the breaks, and winning isn't everything, it's the only thing.

The book was made into a movie last year, and once again pain was the predominant sensation. Nick Nolte acts like a recent graduate of the Kristofferson School of Acting, but past the impassive face is his body, and it is not one to make you jealous. The hurt is there, and it is there more vividly in supporting actor and former football star Tommy Reamon's pulled hamstring. The movie's TV announcers treat these matters, as they have to, as statistics. But Gent's viewpoint makes you realize that these are people. You don't have to feel sorry for these people, who do assume the risk and get well paid, for a while at least, for their efforts. But you do have to think twice about the "game," and wonder how far we have come from the days of the Roman Circus. The TV network that lets stuntmen maim themselves for the new hit show, "That's Incredible," won't do the thinking for you.

Chapter 9
THE STRETCH DRIVE
Is God a Yankee Fan?

Sunday, September 14. The Boston Red Sox have given me so many thrilling moments in the last six years that I do not want to be too hard on them now. For me, Rooster Burleson and Pudge Fisk are the very models of what a major league shortstop and catcher should be. Butch Hobson is a throwback to the storied Twenties, a player who ignores constant pain for the chance to bat in a clutch situation. Fred Lynn is the only centerfielder of the last decade who can stand comparison to the Mays-Mantle-Snider triumvirate. Dewey Evans has kept alive the tradition of a rightfielder with an arm that is a defensive weapon, à la Clemente and Kaline. And Carl Yastrzemski, Captain Carl, is one of the great clutch players of all time, a hero who earned his way into the Hall of Fame in 1967 and is playing with the same determination, albeit not the same body, thirteen years later. So I salute the Red Sox for the successes they have had, for the great team they almost became. And I will not grow bitter over the four games they just lost to the Yankees, or the excruciating fact that in the seven games the two teams played in Boston this year, the Sox didn't win a one.

Each baseball game has its own character, and there is no reason to expect two teams to follow the same script two days in a row. Yet all seven of these games had a depressing sameness: the Yankees got off to an early lead, the Red Sox chipped away for a run here and there to make it close, then Davis or Gossage came in to shut them down in the late innings, preserving a—to take the scores from this weekend—4–2, 4–3 or 5–2 win.

The rational analyst of this pattern would probably cite pitching, which the Yankees have and the Red Sox don't. The emotional analyst might point to a Boston stubbornness that bordered on stupidity. Don Zimmer, no one's favorite manager, called on reliever Bob Stanley to pitch to Bob Watson three games in a row, resulting in two singles, a home run and five RBIs; after proving that Dent and Rodriguez couldn't touch his curve, Dennis Eckersley threw them both inside fastballs, the only pitch they could conceivably hit onto the leftfield screen, which they both did, for four runs and today's victory. Believers in the preternatural, meanwhile, would merely hark back to October 2, 1978, and explain, with ample justification, that the two teams are caught in the mold of the greatest regular-season game ever played, that the Red Sox, like Tantalus, are doomed to come close, but always fall short, for as long as Yaz wears a 6 on his back.

Wednesday, September 17. For the first time in two months, I now vaguely expect to see the Yankees in the 1980 World Series. With a six-game lead over Baltimore and only eighteen games to play, their ascendancy in the AL East is all but assured. But Baltimore, after all, was never much more than a fleeting threat. They created the semblance of a race for about a month, but they never dislodged the Yankees, even temporarily, from first place. My serious hopes all along have been pinned on the Kansas City Royals. But George Brett, the backbone of that team, has been out with tendinitis in his right hand. Starting pitcher Rich Gale, who overpowered the Yankees in the game I saw in Kansas City, has tendinitis in his shoulder. The Royals' winning percentage has dropped to .618, three games off the Yankees' .639 pace. And they will clinch the Western Division title as soon as tomorrow, which will give them two and a half weeks to go stale. The Yankees, meanwhile, will know that they were challenged and they rose to the occasion. The Royals' 8–4 edge in regular-season games was accomplished a long, long time ago. In the last three weeks, I fear, the rest of the Yankee team has watched Gossage and begun to think that they, too, are invincible.

Thursday, September 18. How often can one go to a Yankee-Toronto game and feel sure of seeing the Yankees lose? That was precisely the situation this evening: when we took our seats at 7 o'clock the scoreboard already showed the Blue Jays with a 5–3 lead in the tenth inning. Both teams were still on the field warming up, and they scarcely looked any readier at 7:30 when we sang, after a fashion, "O Canada," and watched play resume where it had been rained out last night. Toronto was still at bat, with nobody on; their two runs had scored when Reggie let a single go through his legs. The first Blue Jay batter hit a ground ball to Dent, who threw wild and looked alibi-ingly at the ground, soft from the first rain in a month. Then Roy Howell hit a single to center and Joe Lefebvre let it go past *him* and the Jays had a 7–3 lead.

Toronto manager Bobby Mattick decided to pick up the three outs needed to finish off the suspended game with his regular-game starter, Dave Steib. Only Steib never picked them up. And furthermore, he never started the regular game. Jackson was nicked by a pitch, Watson walked, Mayberry couldn't hold Dent's line drive and, with two outs, Lefebvre came back from an 0–2 count to walk. No ball had left the infield, yet the Yankees had a run in and the bases loaded. Steib looked desperate, but Mattick didn't move. Steib threw two balls to Randolph, then Randolph lined a drive to right-center. The umpire called him safe at second as Lefebvre, the last and fastest of the baserunners, came home with the tying run. An hour later, Johnny Oates hit a two-out ground-ball single and then scored on Dent's double. The Blue Jays had found a way to lose an unlosable game.

After using his ace unsuccessfully in the suspended game, Mattick reached into obscurity for Luis Leal to start the regular game. Leal had won all of one major league game in his life and had a 6.14 ERA. Is that fair to Baltimore? Is that the kind of competition the Yankees, or any pennant contender, should be getting during the stretch run? Not according to a comment George Steinbrenner made last week when he was having lunch with American League president Lee MacPhail. The league office had sent a memo to all teams, reminding them to use their regular starters against contenders. Steinbrenner said that was a great memo and too bad the Jays weren't starting a strong pitcher that night when they opened against the Orioles. MacPhail passed this on to Toronto's Yankee-hating front office, who told the press and telegrammed a complaint to MacPhail and the Commissioner's office.

One funny thing is that the pitcher Steinbrenner complained about was Paul Mirabella, whose 4–11 record qualified him as a Toronto "regular," and who was strong enough two years ago for Steinbrenner to acquire him from Texas in the Sparky Lyle deal. The second funny thing is that the Commissioner's office announced two days ago that it was actually going to "investigate" the Blue Jays' complaint that Steinbrenner was questioning their integrity. This investigation is about as necessary as last year's inquiry into an autograph-signing session held in the Yankee team bus on a young woman fan's bare bottom. The third funny thing is that if Steinbrenner was serious, tonight's results just showed, once again, how little he (not to mention the Commissioner) understands baseball. Toronto's All-Star pitcher gave up four runs in two-thirds of an inning to give New York a win the

Orioles will never believe, while an absolute unknown pitched a two-hitter to defeat Tommy John, 2–1.

But the last laugh probably belongs to Steinbrenner, who gracefully responded to news of the investigation by calling it "ridiculous, a bad joke." He was just giving the Blue Jays the Clay-Soderholm treatment. It didn't happen to work on Mirabella, who was knocked out in the second inning, but something sure aroused the Blue Jays, who took two games from Baltimore over the weekend, while the Yankees were sweeping Boston. The Yankee lead went from three games to five, and George is probably honing his pop psychology for the Playoffs.

Friday, September 19. Today's bad news is evidence that Reggie Jackson is contagious. With the score tied 1–1 in the bottom of the seventh, Bobby Brown, he of 11 homers and a .243 average, lifted a fastball from Boston's Steve Renko into the rightfield stands. It was not a monumental blast into the bleachers or the upper deck—as a matter of fact, it landed only eight rows behind Dwight Evans, who was standing about 345 feet from home. And it barely stood up as the winning run: Gossage surrendered two hard singles in the ninth before Perez creamed a 3–1 fastball right at Dent for a game-ending doubleplay. But Brown gave it the full Reggie treatment: he dropped the bat at his feet, to mark the spot where the deed was done. Instead of running down to first—always a good idea in case you have misjudged the ball, as Brown often does when he's playing centerfield—he stood tall and admired his handiwork from the batter's box, then *walked* grandly toward first base.

Reggie has patented these moves, and they seemed theatrically appropriate for the 1977 World Series when he hit four home runs in a row and reduced the sixth game itself to a matter of secondary significance. But as Reggie has carried them over into his regular-season act they have become more obnoxious than dramatic. When you are losing 5–2 in the fourth inning and your player hits a home run with no-body on, you want him to circle the bases humbly but with spirit, as if to say, "There's one run back, guys, let's go get the rest"—rather than have him stand there and admire his masterpiece. All that Reggie conveys is the attitude that he's out there for himself, and that regardless of who wins the game, the fans have now gotten their money's worth.

The home-run gloat is a cousin to the uncontested dunk in basketball and the spike in football, both of which, not incidentally, were at one time outlawed in college sports. All three are entertaining, and certainly consistent with societal trends of the last fifteen years. Maybe I'm just old-fashioned, but somehow I would prefer that all this individual expressive-ness develop a vocabulary for saying something other than "Stick it in your face."

Saturday, September 20. Gaylord Perry, Steinbrenner's late-season coup, is giving me a surprising amount of pleasure, on two accounts. First, he is not pitching very well—at least not compared to May, John, Tiant, Guidry, Davis and Gossage—and today his record as a Yankee dropped to 3–3, well off the .694 pace New York has played at since he joined the team. Second, his routine on the mound has revived memories of my all-time favorite National League pitcher, who pitched the Milwaukee Braves to a World Series triumph over the Yan-kees in 1957.

I can't remember what attracted me to the Braves in 1956, but the World Series win of my former favorites, the Dodgers, in 1955 finally removed their underdog status and allowed me to shift my allegiance, mission accomplished. By then I had come to enjoy the oddball status that being a Cleveland fan in the American League gave me and was no doubt looking for a similar team to adopt in the National. For an Indian fan, there was a consistency in also liking the Braves; like me, the franchise was young, having moved its wigwam from Boston in 1953; and unlike the Pirates that my father was pushing on me, the team was good enough for a 10-year-old to stake his nascent reputation on. In 1956 the Braves fell one game short of catching the Dodgers, the Dodgers fell one game short in the World Series against the Yankees, and I doubled my emotional investment in the Braves for 1957.

It was an easy team to love. First baseman Joe Adcock was my hitting idol, a righthanded slugger who hit four home runs and a double in one game and sent balls into remote parts of the Polo Grounds whenever he visited New York. Third baseman Eddie Mathews was a classic lefthanded power hitter, the cover boy on the first issue of *Sports Illustrated,* which was the second thing, after baseball cards, I ever collected. Del Crandall behind the plate and Johnny Logan at short were as solid as their more famous counterparts on the three New York teams. And the outfield of Aaron, Bruton and Covington combined speed, power, youth and an alphabetical primacy that escaped me at the time.

It was also impossible not to cheer for Gene Conley, a goofy-looking 6'8" pitcher who played basketball with the Celtics in the off-season. Warren Spahn was only the greatest pitcher of the '50s. And there were bit players like Andy Pafko, Juan Pizarro (we were studying explorers in school) and Hurricane Hazle. But my favorite of all was Lew Burdette, who had the righthanded delivery, the winning percentage and the he's-number-two obscurity I could root for.

In 1957 the Braves came through with Milwaukee's first pennant, but they were given little chance against the Yankees in the World Series, especially after Ford beat Spahn in the opener. Then Burdette won the second game, and with the Series tied 2–2, he beat Ford 1–0. When the Yankees won the sixth game, Burdette came back with two days' rest and shut out the Yankees again, 5–0, to win the World Series, the car and the tribute of Yankee-haters for all time.

My particular tribute was to adopt the Burdette pitching motion—or more accurately, the nervous mannerisms that preceded each pitch. In rapid succession I would tug at my cap and with my right hand touch my mouth, my chest, my knee, pick up and toss down an imaginary resin bag, and go back up my body in reverse order before starting my windup. At the time, the only breaking pitch I could throw was a wiffle ball, and I didn't imagine that Burdette's routine was anything other than a superstition, of which my other principal ones were tying my shoelaces before each time at bat and picking up some dirt from the batter's box before each pitch. Then Bill White, in a discussion of spitballers (in Perry's honor), mentioned Lew Burdette, and the reason behind the pitching ritual I had innocently adopted suddenly became quite clear.

Where Burdette's routine was vertically aligned, Perry's is horizontal. He starts with the back of his thumb grazing his nose, then the tips of his fingers go to the right and come back across his forehead, just under his cap, sometimes once, sometimes two or three times. Then he brushes the top of his cap's bill, slides his hand around and flicks down the top of his right ear twice and slides back to squeeze the front-center of the bill for punctuation. Sometimes he bends his face down to his left sleeve and comes back and goes through the cap tweaking a second time. And if you still think there is Vaseline somewhere on that cap, well that's fine with Gaylord.

Because of these shenanigans, it takes Perry twice as long to pitch a game as, say, Tommy John. But the Red Sox got rid of him quickly enough today. They hit mostly ground balls in the first two innings, but six of them were good for hits, knocking Gaylord out and bringing in four runs, more than enough this time for Dennis Eckersley, who merely flicks the sweat off his forehead, tugs the bill of his cap, touches the back of his cap and tugs the bill again before each pitch.

Sunday, September 21. The Yankees finished off a 10–3 year against the Red Sox today in a dull game decided in the first inning, when all the runs in New York's 3–0 win came home. Some ever vigilant statistician pointed out that this loss mathematically eliminated Boston from the 1980 division race. That's nothing. "In the sweep of four games [last weekend]," according to the *Boston Globe,* "the Yankees put an end to the era 1975 supposedly began. With this final degradation, the Yankees finished five years of beating the Red Sox *any time they had to.*"

And just as the Yankees dominated the opposition on the field, their traveling circus held sway in the off-the-field arena, and the *Globe,* for once, was not too proud to send a reporter to cover it. *Globe* columnist Leigh Montville interviewed the twenty fans who hung around the lobby of the Sheraton Boston for Yankee autographs their first day in town. Not all players cooperate in this ritual, and in fairness to their point of view, these kids are not looking for a once-in-a-lifetime thrill; they are more professional pests, who will sell any extra autographs they can get. Still, the difference in players' attitudes would be instructive if it weren't so expected. The nicest team, according to this article, is the Orioles; they will sign anything, over and over. At the other extreme is former Yankee pitching coach Art Fowler. "He told me to go play in the traffic," one young fan said.

The biggest game of all, no surprise, is Reggie Jackson. "He just signs 'Reggie' most of the time," complained one expert, without speculating whether that's to annoy the collectors or simply to indicate his greatness. This day, when he descended from the coffee shop, he was in control. He told the youthful entrepreneurs that he was signing once this trip, today was it, and he did not want to see any of the same faces for the rest of the weekend. "You got it?!" As 14-year-old Keith Nashawaty explained: "You have to get Reggie when he's feeling good. He said to me once, 'Do you know I have to do this every day of my life?' I told him, 'Reggie, a guy has an obligation to his fans.' He looked at me and said, 'Not to you, kid.'"

Monday, September 22. One of the acknowledged beauties of baseball is that, no matter how many games you see, in any given game you are likely to witness something you have never seen before. And if you are luckier than I was tonight, it won't cost your team the game.

Watching the Cleveland Indians play at Yankee Stadium has provided me my share of disappointment. How well I remember last October, when Billy Martin brought in Goose Gossage in the ninth expressly to humiliate Cliff Johnson, the man who broke the Goose's thumb in the shower. To my amazed pleasure, Johnson lined an RBI double to give Cleveland the lead—until Oscar Gamble hit a three-run pinch homer to return the Tribe, and me, to the depression that goes with a sixth-place finish. On our first meeting this season, Cleveland led a high-scoring game until the bottom of the ninth, when New York pulled out an 11–10 win. I am faithful to my adopted favorites, however, and when the Tribe arrived for their last visit of 1980 to the Apple, there I was, sitting behind their dugout, matching the beefy bodies and long hair to the names I had been following in box scores over the summer.

The beefiest body belonged to Indian starting pitcher Len Barker, a 6′5″ fireballer who came up with the Texas Rangers and who now, at the age of 25, is threatening to become the first Clevelander since Sudden Sam McDowell in 1970 to lead the league in strikeouts. Watching him for the first time, I was glad to see that Barker had an old-fashioned high-kick delivery. Bobby Brown was glad to see it, too, and he stole second after a walk, the 47th steal in 55 attempts against Barker. Brown made it 48 in the fourth, went on to third on the wild throw and scored on Watson's sacrifice fly. Barker was pitching a no-hitter and losing the game, 1–0, which was an early sign that it was not Cleveland's night.

The Tribe scraped up runs off Tommy John in the fifth and sixth for a 2–1 lead going into the bottom of the eighth. Then for the fourth time, Barker walked the leadoff batter of an inning and displayed suicidal tendencies by putting the lead run on as well. Brown drove in one run with a bad-hop double over the first baseman, and Watson made the score 4–2 with a Baltimore chop over the drawn-in infield. It was the kind of attack you read about in Greek mythology, where a goddess intervenes to direct an arrow's flight.

In came Gossage to pitch the ninth, and Jack Brohamer pinch-hit a single to right. With the count 3–1 on Toby Harrah, Cleveland manager Garcia sent out a pinch runner—an attempt to delay the game and break Gossage's rhythm. It worked and Harrah walked. After a sacrifice bunt Rick Manning delivered one run with a ground-out. Harrah, now on third with the potential tying run, made a mad dash halfway down the line toward home. The fake steal of home is something we all learned in Baserunning 101. The move, however, is usually as successful as squaring around to bunt on the 3–0 pitch, and most mature players cannot be bothered with the tactic. The part of the lesson that always gets underlined, however, is the warning to take your lead in foul territory, because if you're hit with a batted ball in fair territory, you're out. It's a nice theoretical lesson, but the odds that the batter will (1) swing and (2) hit a ball (3) down the third-base line (4) that the runner can't avoid are so long that, like so much else we were taught in school, it is not something we worry about once the exam is over. Imagine my surprise, imagine the Yankees' surprise, imagine Harrah's surprise, when lefthanded pinch hitter Ron Hassey lined a fair ball down the third-base line, where it bounced off Harrah's hip for the Indians' tenth hit and twenty-seventh out. It was an ending no one had seen before. And if there is an Olympus, someone up there must be smiling.

Tuesday, September 23. Lord have mercy on a poor Cleveland fan like me. The Indians had the game won, locked up, in the bag, ahead 4–1 in the bottom of the ninth. Then Wayne Garland *walked Bucky Dent* and God's will was quickly done:

six batters later, Eric Soderholm drove in Brown and Watson's pinch runner to end the game, 5–4. If I have updated the source of divine intervention responsible for the Cleveland defeats, it is at the suggestion of hitting hero Soderholm, who explained the secret of the Yankees' success in a postgame radio interview: "I think God's a Yankee fan this year." This wouldn't surprise me or the Time Inc. spokesman who cracked last week that rooting for the Yankees was like rooting for God or General Motors. And as everyone knows from watching the Goose charioted in from the bullpen in a pinstriped Toyota, the Yankees have updated the automotive third of the trinity as well.

The Indians don't give up like the Red Sox when they play New York. On Monday they were the first team to score off Gossage in a month. Tonight Harrah bounced back from his goatdom to drive in three runs in the first three innings, knocking out Rudy May. But if you want to beat the Yankees, you don't walk Bucky Dent. Pitch underhand if you have to, let him hit the ball out of his hand, but don't walk Dent. This is the first and great commandment. And the second is like unto it: if your pitcher walks Dent, take him out of the game.

Barker had a two-hitter when he walked Dent to open the eighth on Monday. Take him out, I told Garcia, though only my father sitting next to me heard. My advice was ignored for four more batters, by which time Cleveland's 2–1 lead had been transformed into a 4–2 deficit. The very next night, Garland, with a 4–1 lead, started the ninth by walking Dent, by now in an 0-for-17 slump. The handwriting on the wall was so clear only a blind man or a Cleveland manager could fail to see it. When Garland also walked pinch hitter Murcer, the Yankee comeback was inevitable. Brown and Watson each drove in runs. Thankful for small favors, I listened as Reggie grounded out to first. Thankful for big favors, I heard that the Orioles came back with a three-run eighth to top Boston, 8–6. In total despair, I heard Soderholm hit a ball up the alley. Even Frank Messer was excited. And the

Biggest Yankee Fan had consigned me to another night in my own private purgatory.

Wednesday, September 24. For a baseball team that is covered by the largest, nosiest and most creative concentration of media in the daily sports world, the Yankees are surprisingly short of nicknames. There is "Chicken" Stanley, "Goose" Gossage, "Bull" Watson and "Puff" Nettles, and Guidry has three or four all by himself. But if Dent, Randolph, Spencer, Murcer, Jones, Brown, John, May or Underwood have monikers, they have slipped by me. Of all the nicknames, far and away the most inappropriate belongs to "Sweet Lou" Piniella, who was officially reprimanded yesterday by AL president Lee MacPhail for on-field rudeness. As Rizzuto often explains, the "Sweet" refers to Lou's swing, not his personality.

Lou is always near the top of the league when it comes to throwing helmets and kicking water coolers. Earlier this year he directed every obscenity in the book at fans behind the Yankee dugout who generously offered him a suggestion on how to end his batting slump ("Take yourself out, Lou"). And his conduct in the rainy Oakland game I went to last month has now prompted this unusual and undoubtedly ineffectual response from the Principal's Office. Piniella warmed up in the second inning by kicking, screaming and skimming his batting helmet a good 90 feet when the third-base umpire called him out for fan interference on a dropped foul popup. Then after doubling, singling and seeing his team take a 5–1 lead, Lou hit a ball to rightfield that should have been caught but wasn't. When official scorer Harold Rosenthal, a retired baseball writer, scored the play an error, Sweet Lou, on second base, raised his arms and gestured in disbelief toward the press box, and he continued to attack the scorer in his postgame remarks. The fact that the Yankees had won a game in a hot pennant race was quite beside the point.

His temper aside, Lou is in many ways the consummate Yankee. He belonged to five teams and played five full years in Kansas City before the Yankees got him in a one-sided trade (for Lindy McDaniel) in 1973. He appears in blue jean ads (Sasson) with pretty girls. He is articulate and handles himself well (complains freely) with the press. He's individualistic, short on the rah-rah, and when the season's on the line in September, he's a professional hitter. And as much as Piniella's concern for himself bothers me, it's impossible to boo the guy—as the object of the only special cheer the Yankee fans have, "Looooooo" is boo-proof.

Wednesday, September 24. After those two heartbreaking setbacks, Cleveland suffered a routine loss tonight, 7–3. It didn't bother me, because I was at the movies. In the words of Doug DeCinces, call in the dogs, put out the fire, the hunt is over. The Magic Number, that reduction of all of baseball's wondrous complexity to a single digit, is 6, which is one fewer than the numbers of games the Yankees have remaining with the Detroit Tigers. If New York plays .500 ball the next ten days, the Orioles would have to go undefeated to catch them.

But before I get so upset by the pennant-winning hysteria that I have to take a week off from baseball altogether, let me give a Yankee-hating salute to the Baltimore Orioles, who have played the most courageous and exciting baseball of the year and have created a pennant race where by all rights none should exist. Or as Bucky Dent said earlier in the week, "This is ridiculous. We've won 95 games and we're still scuffling."

To look at the figures first, the Orioles now have the second-best record in all of baseball; they, not Kansas City, should be the second team to register 100 wins—only the second time in twenty-five years an AL team has won 100 games and not a pennant or division title. They have won 17 of 24 games in September—and in the process have lost 3½ games to the Yankees. Their last encounter with the Yankees on the field was August 18; since then they have had to play two games every day—one against a live opponent on the field, the other against the absent Yankees on the scoreboard.

Their manner of victory has been dramatic. Friday, De-Cinces emerged from Weaver's doghouse (which he had been sharing with the dogs he prematurely called in) to hit a twelfth-inning home run that beat the Jays, 8–6. Sunday the Birds won 2–1 when catcher Rick Dempsey picked the tying run off second base with two out in the ninth. When the Red Sox went ahead 6–5 in the eighth Tuesday night, the Orioles came back with three runs for an 8–6 win. Then on Wednesday, Boston KO'd 24-game-winner Steve Stone with six runs in the first two innings, only to have Baltimore tie the game in the bottom of the third and win 12–9 on Terry Crowley's seventh-inning homer.

I hope, for the sake of their pride, that the Orioles do not give up now, just because I have.

Thursday, September 25. If Rick Waits can't beat Gaylord Perry, I'll pack it in. After three losses in a row to the Yankees, not only is the law of averages on our side, but Howser is giving half his team a rest. He is starting nine righthanders against the Indians' Yankee-killing lefty, in the kind of total platooning that worked so poorly for the late Gene Mauch at Minnesota this year.

Waits remained my hero with the sixth win in his last seven decisions against the Yankees, and the Magic Number rested at 6.

Friday, September 26. The Orioles jumped off to a 1–0 lead and I thought, if the Yanks can lose to Detroit, the lead will be 3½ —not insurmountable with nine games to play. Soderholm's grand slam in the Yankee third interrupted my dream. Then Ricky Peters's triple with no outs cut the Yankee lead to 6–5. But Trammell and Kemp struck out and Detroit wound up losing, 7–5. Baltimore scored two runs in the ninth but came up on the short end of a 5–4 score in Cleveland. The Magic Number dropped sharply to 4.

Saturday, September 27. My position in the stretch run is untenable, for not only must I root for the Yankees to lose every one of their remaining seven games, I must hope that the Orioles can win theirs—even though half their games are against Cleveland. A true Yankee-hater would sacrifice his team, even at those long odds, but some Orioles flattened the beer when they gracelessly attacked the Tribe for blowing that 4–1 lead in the eighth inning Tuesday night. (Sammy Stewart: "Let's send a Candygram to Cleveland and blow the town up." Frank Robinson: "Don't do them any favors.") This not only diminished my admiration for Baltimore's effort, it made the Indians ripping mad. And they have taken out their anger by plucking the Birds twice in a row. Baltimore's 6–5 loss to Cleveland today nullified the good work of Jack Morris and the Tigers, who ended Tommy John's Cy Young hopes, 5–1. The Magic Number eased to 3.

Sunday, September 28. My perseverance in front of the TV set paid off today and I got to watch, for the first time all year, another team use late-inning home runs to beat the Yankees. The Yanks were cruising with a 3–0 lead over Detroit when Lance Parrish hit a two-out three-run homer off Ron Davis, ending his twenty-inning string of scoreless innings. The Yankees regained the lead 5–3 until Champ Summers hit the first home run Goose Gossage has allowed since July 26. Rather than risk tiring Gossage, Howser let Mike Griffin start the tenth. He still hasn't gotten anyone out. With the bases loaded, Bob Watson tried to turn a grounder into a first-and-home doubleplay without catching the ball first, and the Tigers registered a gutsy 6–5 win. Baltimore beat the Indians, and the Magic Number sits at 3.

If the Yankees are to clinch the division title in the coming week, it will not be with me watching. The local television stations are not scheduled to broadcast any baseball games during the final week of the season, and I listened sadly today as both Met and Yankee announcers said good-bye to their TV audiences, marking, for me, the official end of summer. (Frank, Bill and the Scooter did give a rather tentative farewell, as they will be resurrected for the Playoffs if the Yankees make it.) By thus ignoring the season's final week, Channels 9 and 11 are, in effect, the last holdouts honoring a great baseball tradition: the 154-game season.

The old schedule, which lasted for 57 years from 1904 through 1960, was a symmetrical beauty: each team played every other team in the 8-team league 22 times, 11 at home and 11 away. This was the schedule over which the modern standards we still use to judge a player's achievement were forged: 20 wins and 200 strikeouts are the magic marks for a pitcher, 200 hits and 100 RBIs are the tests of a batter. When Roger Maris needed 162 games in 1961 to break baseball's most famous mark, Babe Ruth's 60 home runs in a season, the longer season was a burning issue. But each year since then there has been less and less acknowledgment that it isn't quite fair to compare today's quantitative marks with those of yesteryear.

Out of respect for those old days I bought the Sunday *Times* today. That paper is thicker than ever and even the news pages are more full of announcements than news, but the sports section carried the complete major league stats through Friday night, the 154-game point for exactly half the teams (most of the others caught up over the weekend). This year the category that stands to be diluted the most is 20-game winners in the American League. While Stone, John and Oakland's Mike Norris are legitimately there, the extra eight games will give McGregor, Leonard, Barker, Langford and conceivably Gura a shot at joining a club that will have only one member, Steve Carlton, in the National League.

Ty Cobb is one of the biggest losers in this devaluation, mainly because he had so many records in the first place. Last year Pete Rose, in his 158th game of the season, got his

200th hit for the tenth time in his career, breaking a record Cobb set between 1907 and 1924. Kudos to Rose, who is the closest we have to a Cobb today, but let's also note that if Rose had been playing 154-game seasons, Cobb's record, according to my calculations, would be unchallenged. This year Cobb lost his American League stolen-base record, which had stood sixty-five years. Rickey Henderson stole four bases yesterday in Oakland's 156th game of the year, tying him with the Georgia Peach at 96, with six games still to play. Of course, the 21-year-old Henderson may obliterate the record within 154 games in the future once he learns how to run the bases, but for now I'll give him an asterisk.

Monday, September 29. The Birds may be dead but they're not yet buried, and their 5–2, 4–3 doubleheader win over the Red Sox tonight brought them within 3½ games of the Yankees, who had the day off. The Yankees' 2-game series starting tomorrow in Cleveland becomes that much more important, and it is conceivable that the Tribe could throw Waits and Barker at them. The Magic Number stays at 3, but that 3 is looming larger.

Tuesday, September 30.

> *Listen, my friends, and you shall hear*
> *Of the greatest game of the Yankees' year.*
>
> *The visiting Bombers jumped off fast*
> *With two quick runs on a Reggie blast.*
>
> *But Cleveland scored eight when it came to bat;*
> *With Rick Waits pitching, I thought, "That's that."*
>
> *(Baltimore added its part to my fun:*
> *After five in Boston, the Birds led 10–1.)*
>
> *Then a triple by Brown and a single by Dent*
> *Scored runs in the fourth and out Waits went.*

A homer by Eric and a single by Lou
In the fifth gave the Yanks another two.

The Yankees went wild and I fell to earth
On a three-run homer by pinch hitter Werth.

There were three frames to go, but what was the use?
With a 9–8 lead, Howser brought in the Goose.

But Bannister singled, Cerone passed a ball,
On the Indian bench, Charboneau got the call.

Super Joe couldn't run, but still he had pride:
A hit up the middle—the ballgame was tied!

Hargrove and Hassey drove in three more,
The Yanks' Goose was cooked, like never before.

New York celebrated too early this time;
I had the last laugh, the Tribe won, 12–9.

Excuse the bad poem, forgive me my glee,
The Yanks' Magic Number's still resting at 3.

Wednesday, October 1. A. M. Three years ago Time Inc. sued the New York Yankees, Commissioner Bowie Kuhn and New York Mayor Abe Beame to force the Yankees to allow women reporters into the players' locker room on the same basis as men. A *Sports Illustrated* reporter named Melissa Ludtke had asked Dodger manager Tom Lasorda and player rep Tommy John for locker room access the day before the 1977 World Series opened in New York. The Dodgers took a vote and the majority said okay, but when Ludtke alerted the locker room guard, he told the Dodger publicity man, who told the Commissioner's representative, who told the Yankees' publicity man to tell Ludtke during the game, "No way." In the lawsuit that followed, the Yankees contributed canned affidavits from Billy Martin, Bob Lemon, Graig Nettles and Dick Tidrow, all referring to the locker room as the place where players "attend to personal hygiene." Martin also contributed the interesting argument that "players' wives would be deeply offended if other women were present" in the locker room. But the laboring oar was pulled by our friends at the Commissioner's office, whose principal argument was that baseball was "America's family game, the game that bridges the generation gap," and that "to permit members of the opposite sex into this place of privacy . . . would be to undermine the basic dignity of the game."

I was somewhere in the rearguard on the women-in-the-locker-room issue, although my opposition to this particular bit of progress was not based on the absurd position espoused by the Commissioner and summarily rejected by the federal court. First, I happen to like the atmosphere of an all-male locker room. We still have a ways to go before male athletes will behave in the same manner with women present—and I'm not sure we should ever get to that point, either. Second, I can't get past the logical impasse posed by the reverse situation: no one is seriously suggesting that male sportswriters be allowed into women's locker rooms. Third, there is nothing unreasonable in treating the press like the general public. If a player's brother or father can come in, but his sister and mother are excluded, then it's fair to let in male reporters and not female reporters. Women reporters will have a corresponding advantage covering Nancy Lopez and Chris Evert. If women's sports are not so newsworthy—well, that's a difference, not discrimination.

Fourth, locker room reporting is overdone anyway, and the modern trend in this direction should be discouraged rather than enshrined as a constitutional right. A manager, who's in a separate room anyway, may shed light on his strategy, but if any player ever made a comment that illuminated the game just played, I can't remember it. In assessing the state of the Yankees after the dramatic, if not poetic, loss to the Indians last night, three of New York's daily papers relied on an intimate description of Gossage's shaving himself with a razor after the game. For the *Times* and the *Post,* the point seemed to be that the Yankees were not about to slit their throats, while for *Newsday* the point was that Goose's slump was so bad "he left some hairs on his face." I have never been in the Yankee locker room after a game, but Melissa Ludtke now has, after winning her suit, and she told me how the mass of reporters moves around the room like a swarm of bees, with as many as fifteen reporters leaning over each other's shoulders to hear a player's response. Probably the real invasion of privacy is not in having a woman in the room as you change out of your uniform, but in having reporters of every paper in town, regardless of sex, staring at you and the mirror as you shave, not letting you forget that you just pitched your worst game of the year.

Wednesday, October 1. P.M. The Yankees got back on the track tonight and moved the Magic Number down to 2 with an 18–7 win over Barker and the Tribe. Eighteen is the most runs scored by the Yankees since 1974, and let me tell you how they got that 18th. The Yankees led 12–0 after three innings, so the game was not exactly close. By the ninth inning, the Yankees led 17–5 and Perry was in for John, Doyle was in for Randolph, Stanley was in for Dent, Spencer was in for Watson, Lefebvre was in for Gamble, Oates was in for Cerone, and Marshall Brandt, the International League's MVP, had had his first major league at-bat (a strikeout). But who was still playing rightfield? Look at the date. And what was he doing there? Trying to regain the American League home-run lead. Reggie Jackson was the only Yankee to bat six times during the rout, and with nobody on in the ninth he hit one out for the Yankees' 18th run. I should have kept track this year of how many Reggie homers have been meaningful and how many meaningless. I suspect that two-thirds fall into the latter category—and of those, none can top the one tonight.

Thursday, October 2. The Yankees resorted to some familiar weapons—the pitching of Guidry and Gossage, home runs by Gamble and Jackson—to beat the Tigers 3–2 and whittle the Magic Number to 1. For the second straight day in October, Reggie got credit for the game-winning RBI, after not having had one since the last time he discussed the subject. By old-fashioned reckoning, however, the winning run (the third run) scored in the sixth when Gamble left third too early on Watson's sacrifice fly to right and the umpire didn't have the guts to call him out.

Just to show how bitter, mean, vile and despicably low a person I am, I hope that the Yankees' clincher comes on a Baltimore loss to Cleveland, not a Yankee win. I won't begrudge them their champagne, I just want it to come in through the back door and taste a little sour.

Friday, October 3. The Royal Screw of the Year Award goes to umpire Bill Haller, who called off tonight's game in the fifth inning with the Tigers leading the Yankees, 4–0. I mean, Lancegate and Billygate absolutely *pale* next to this scandal, and if Earl Weaver wasn't already suing Haller for secretly wearing a live mike during a Weaver tirade last month, he would have grounds to lodge a complaint tonight.

It was raining when the game started, but there were 35,000 fans at the Stadium and George has a shot at setting the American League season attendance record. The Tigers scored two runs in the top of the first, one on an error by Jackson, and they added another in the second. In the fourth the rain came a little harder, the umps started conferring with each other, and Reggie struck out with Gamble on base for the second time. Sensing a loss coming, the Yankees directed their attention at the rain. Underwood acted as if it were humanly impossible to pitch from the wet mound, although his Tiger counterpart, Dan Petry, was throwing a shutout. Reggie pointedly stayed in the dugout holding his bat when it was his turn to be on deck. Rodriguez let a ground ball slip out of his hands twice for the Yankees' third error. And Bob Watson made the ultimate sacrifice: he took himself out of the game in the fourth, claiming there was too much rain on his glasses for him to see the ball. When the Tigers scored yet again in the fifth, and Howser came slowly out to change pitchers, the umps called for the tarpaulin.

They've gone this far, I thought, they'll definitely get at least one more inning in somehow, even though it may take a couple of hours. Since WPIX had decided, with Steinbrenner's last-minute approval, to televise the title-clinching game, I was following developments closely on my usual Friday night rounds at the office. Waiting till midnight, or even later, for a Yankee loss would be no hardship for me. When I looked out the window at 11:00 the rain had stopped and I turned the TV back on. No game. Imagine my utter astonishment fifteen minutes later when I heard Warner Wolf on the news say the game had been rained out, and there would be a doubleheader Saturday instead. I looked out the window again —still no umbrellas. I was up for two more hours, and there was still no more rain, just an occasional light mist.

There was room for debate whether the game should have been started at all. But once it started, and especially once it went into the fifth inning, the unwritten rule is, unless the rain gets much worse, you get the game in. And to call the game for good at 10:30, after waiting only fifty-five minutes, indicates a suspiciously quick trigger. The Yankees had made their feelings quite evident—from the moment they fell behind. Reggie even stopped to discuss the situation with the umpires on his way in from rightfield as the ground crew placed the tarp, although that may have been just a camera-baiting move. By this point, the only people who weren't complaining about the rain were the Tigers. Of course, they don't have to worry because, unlike the struggling Yankees, they have already clinched fifth place.

P.S. Weaver took the news quite calmly: "I don't care if it's a monsoon, not one other umpire in baseball would have called it. . . . Okay, so it probably won't make a difference, but it's a joke. George Steinbrenner got Bill Haller to do exactly what George Steinbrenner wanted and you can quote me on that. . . . This guy [Haller] has been doing some of the most unbelievable, ungodly things I have ever seen. I'm wondering if he's sick. . . . I hope to have Steinbrenner ousted as American League president this winter and get somebody other than him running the league next year."

Saturday, October 4. The division title was clinched as it had to be: Reggie hit a dramatic three-run, game-winning home run, Goose struck out the side in the ninth, and the Scooter yelled "Holy cow!" For all the drama, there wasn't much pressure. It was the first game of a doubleheader, and if worse came to worse, the Orioles themselves had to play a doubleheader in the evening against the Indians. The Tigers were starting Roger Weaver, a rookie with a lifetime major league record of 3–3. And if this game got away, New York had Tiant and John ready to start the next two. Detroit's "success" in last night's rainout even stacked the law of averages against them. Overall, the odds were so terrible that I decided not to stick around and watch. If somehow the Yankees could lose two and the Orioles win two, then there would be something to watch on Sunday.

I made the right move. I would have suffered too much watching Randolph lead off the game with another walk— the worst omen of all. The Tigers' 2–1 lead in the fourth would have been just enough to raise false hopes. And when with two on, two out, and the score tied 2–2, Reggie Jackson levitated his 41st home run into the upper deck in right, and waited for the ball to hit the seats before he moved from the batter's box, I would have died, or done something worse. The Tigers continued to get men on base against Gossage, but that proved the vainest hope of all. With 55,000 fans screaming and the title there for the clinching, Gossage was pumped up and final batter Hebner didn't have a chance.

But forty-six miles up the Hudson River, just before Goose threw the last strike, I watched the clock run out at Michie Stadium with the Harvard football team upset victors over Army, 15–10. I quietly put my transistor radio back under our lunch box from Zabar's and, under the beautiful late-afternoon sun at West Point, considered my day a success.

Sunday, October 5. The Dodgers beat the Astros on ABC to force a sudden-death playoff tomorrow, but for everyone else the 1980 regular season ended today, making this the best day of the year for the statistics-minded baseball fan. And not only are statistics something fans love to collect, re-arrange and compare, the ballplayers and their managers love to create them. Ron LeFlore has been sidelined with a broken wrist for three weeks, but he stuck around to pinch-run in the Expos' pennant drive. That ended Saturday, but today, in a meaningless game, LeFlore pinch-ran and stole two bases to pass the Pirates' Omar Moreno, 97–96, and become the first player in history to win stolen-base titles in both the American and National Leagues. Steve Garvey bunted for his 200th hit—the only National Leaguer to reach that plateau this year and the sixth time Garvey has done it—putting him one year ahead of Pete Rose's pace. Bill Buckner of the Cubs passed Gary Templeton over the weekend for the first time this year and won the NL batting crown with a .324 average, which would have been good for eighth place in the suddenly statistically superior American League. And Cleveland's Len Barker put away the strikeout crown with 188 in an other-wise miserable final-day outing against the Orioles, losing 7–1 to give Baltimore its 100th win of the year. Mike Norris, who had been one strikeout behind Barker, didn't pitch today be-cause Billy Martin preferred to give Rick Langford a second shot at his 20th win.

But none of these assaults on the record book need take a back seat to what happened at Yankee Stadium, where Mr. October entered the meaningless final game against the Tigers .0013 short of hitting .300 for the first time in his statistically illustrious career. All credit to Reggie, his first time up he sliced a triple to left that Steve Kemp dove for and missed and then scored on Soderholm's home run before Howser got confirmation from the press box that Reggie was at .300—well, actually .2996—and could be taken out of the game. And since those two runs in the second held up for a 2–1 win, I suppose it is being petty of me to note that Reggie's personal quest resulted in the Yankees' having Ted Wilborn batting in the cleanup spot from the third inning on.

But I didn't come out a complete loser on the Reggie front this week. Four hours after Reggie ended his season, in the bottom of the ninth in Milwaukee, Ben Oglivie hit his 41st homer to tie the game, spoil Langford's bid, and most importantly, force Reggie to share the 1980 American League home-run crown.

Chapter 10
THE PLAYOFFS
A Royal Revenge

Wednesday, October 8. 9:00 A.M. This is the day I have been
waiting for since July. Today is the day for pressure baseball.
Today we will see if the Yankees are champions or are merely,
as I suspect, the best of a mediocre lot. The Yankees did not
do well in pressure games during the year. They lost the
season series to both of their chief competitors, Kansas City
and Baltimore. The Royals absolutely destroyed New York,
but the Yankees are now unanimously saying those games
didn't mean very much. What did? The games against Seattle?
The Yankees beat the Orioles in April—were those the important games?—but lost six of eight in August, in the closest
thing to a showdown we saw all year. The Yankees can't even
claim that they responded to the pressure of clinching the
division title. With the Magic Number at 6, they lost four out
of five games to Detroit and Cleveland; they managed to play
.500 ball over the last eleven days of the season only because
a sure loss was rained out in the fifth inning.

And yet the Yankees are acting like they are the favorites —and the Royals seem to be going right along. When Kansas City clinched the Western Division title way back on September 17, they were already worried about the Yankees. "That's only half the job," cautioned rightfielder Clint Hurdle. "That's why I want the Yankees. We win, they win and let's find out the story." George Brett agreed: "It would be good for baseball, good for this team and good for this city if we beat the Yankees. It's not vengeance. It's just wanting to regroup and regain your pride and self-respect."

It made me nervous to hear a man batting .396 for a team with a 17½-game lead speak of "regrouping" and "regaining self-respect." The Royals didn't make me feel any better when, after clinching their division, they spun into an eight-game losing streak against Oakland, Seattle and Minnesota. And Larry Gura, their starting pitcher in the Playoffs and a Cy Young candidate in August, couldn't get past his 18th win in the last five weeks of the season.

On the other hand, Kansas City snapped their losing streak in style a week ago when Brett hit a three-run fourteenth-inning homer, and they proceeded to win five of their last six games. Their hitters warmed up on Saturday with a 17–1 romp over the Twins, and pitchers Splittorff and Gale combined on a 4–0 shutout in the season finale. Willie Wilson finally got thrown out, after 32 consecutive stolen bases, but he ended the season leading the majors in triples (15), runs (134) and hits (230). With the pressure of reaching .400 and worrying about his injured hand finally off, Brett went 9-for-18 in his last five games and accomplished the extraordinary feat (last accomplished in 1950, by Walt Dropo) of knocking in more runs (a team record 118) than he had games played (117).

Looking just at season statistics, the Royals have a decided edge in hitting, the Yankees a similarly large edge in pitching. Kansas City has a huge edge in team speed, which gives them an advantage both on the bases and in the field. New York has more power. Dan Quisenberry and Gossage tied for the league lead in saves (a suspect statistic), but I didn't like to hear Hurdle refer to the Goose yesterday as "the master of disaster." The artificial turf of Royals Stadium, where the first two games will be played, gives Kansas City another edge because it accentuates the Yankees' weak outfield defense and the limited range of the left side of their infield.

That is why this first game is so important. If Kansas City comes out spraying doubles, the Yankees will be off balance and may never recover. If New York can hold the Royals close—or, heaven forbid, even win the game—New York's psychological dominance may become the key factor. It is true that there are many new players on both sides since the battles of '76, '77 and '78. Perhaps even more importantly, there are two new managers. I am not worried about Brett or the other Royal hitters, except to the extent that I am always worried about Otis in a clutch situation. But it is the Kansas City pitchers who have had good year after good year and have failed in the Playoffs to hold the Yankees, and I am sure that they remember.

I saw last year, in an otherwise unimportant game, what this memory can do. It was August 1979, and Paul Splittorff had a three-hitter and a 2–1 lead over Tommy John going into the ninth, in Kansas City. With two strikes on Murcer, Splittorff lost a pitch and hit him. Piniella hit a broken-bat single, and another inside pitch nicked Chambliss. Late-inning Yankee rallies from the past had crept up from his subconscious and when he glanced at the dugout, you knew his confidence was gone. Not only did Roy White and Fred Stanley then drive in five runs, but the dispirited Royals went down 1-2-3 in the bottom of the ninth. If Wilson, Washington, Porter and Wathan don't give Splittorff, Gura, Leonard and Gale the big leads they provided during the season, I am afraid that those pitchers, in a close ninth inning, will have a hard time forgetting the past.

Wednesday, October 8. 2:00 P.M. George Steinbrenner has used his arrival in Kansas City to watch the Playoffs as a forum to suggest that the American League switch to a three-division alignment in 1982. "It's better for the fans to keep more cities alive for the Playoffs and better economically," he noted. The Playoffs would become a four-team affair, with semifinals and finals, featuring the three division winners and the ever popular "wild card," the second-place team with the best percentage. With a wild card, George argued, good teams like this year's Orioles, last year's Brewers and the 1978 Red Sox would not be shut out of postseason play.

This last, however, is precisely the argument *against* wild cards. The 1978 Yankee–Red Sox final game was so great because everything was on the line; if the loser gets into the Playoffs anyway, what's the big deal? And what there was of a pennant race with the Orioles this year would have disappeared with three weeks left in the season, when the Birds assured themselves of the best second-place finish.

The three-division split-up itself is a made-for-TV concept that can have no real appeal to baseball fans or to the players, either. Everyone I know wants to go back to single divisions with eight teams, rather than move in the opposite direction. While that may be unrealistic, the competitive problem that the American League has is not at the top of the divisions, but at the bottom. Creating one more division would not help the situation in Toronto or Seattle. And for the players, their goal is to get into the World Series, not the Playoffs.

It's not surprising that this kind of moneymaking idea should appeal to Steinbrenner or that he could care less about baseball's greatest strength, its tradition. What worries me is that more and more of the new baseball owners seem to share

Steinbrenner's ignorance of real baseball values, and for some a baseball franchise is merely another investment in fame, no different from the basketball or soccer franchise they also hold. They may see playoffs as the financial jackpot in America's other pro sports leagues and say, why not in baseball? If so, they don't understand that baseball is the only sport in which the regular season still means something, and that a baseball fan can therefore consider his team's season a success even if it doesn't make the Playoffs.

I am hoping that this particular proposal is doomed because the National League, with two fewer teams and far more competitive divisions, won't go along and will refuse to sit idly by while the American has an extra round of playoffs. The National League is the last bastion of baseball tradition, the big-league refuge of the pure, nine-man game of baseball. This year's National League vote to reject the designated-hitter rule, which I have come to terms with but not to favor, was nevertheless close enough for concern. So long as new attendance records are set each year, the economics don't support those who say the fans just want to see more hitting. But the curve can't go up forever, and when it stops, what will keep men like George Steinbrenner, who show so little heed for society's rules, from tampering with those of baseball?

Wednesday, October 8. 7:00 P.M. The Royals didn't play terribly well this afternoon, but the Yankees actually gave runs away, and the myth of Yankee postseason invincibility should now be heavily discounted—at least until this Playoff series goes to a fifth game. The Kansas City game plan was to keep Gossage off the mound and it worked, as the Royals got two runs in the second, two in the third, one in the seventh and two in the eighth for an easy 7–2 win.

It didn't look so easy in the top of the second inning when Larry Gura hung curves to Cerone and Piniella and they hit consecutive home runs down the leftfield line. Gura at that point looked terrible, and you had to wonder why Kansas City was starting a pitcher who was 0–5 with a 6.46 ERA the last month of the season. He ended up allowing ten hits, but no more runs, in a very gutsy complete-game performance. The key was his success against Mr. October, who swung the bat like he did in September: he made the third out three times and stranded baserunners in each of his four at-bats, three in scoring position. Reggie, who for some as yet unannounced reason did not shave today, was the only lefthanded bat in the Yankee lineup, and Kansas City manager Jim Frey undoubtedly preferred this lineup to the one he knew he would get if he brought righthanded reliever Renie Martin in for Gura. Of what use was the Yankee depth when Murcer, Spencer, Gamble and the reactivated Nettles stayed on the bench, and the final three outs of the game were made by Rodriguez, Brown and Dent?

What really killed the Yankees, and disappointed any fans looking for championship-caliber baseball, was their defensive generosity. A single, walk and wild pitch by Guidry put two men in scoring position in the second, whence they scored when Piniella wanted Dent to take Frank White's Texas Leaguer while Bucky was getting out of Lou's way. Another walk and a hard double by Otis put ducks on the pond once more the next inning for Willie Aikens, who was 0-for-12 lifetime with seven strikeouts against Guidry, and I asked myself, what's he doing in the lineup? But Aikens sliced the 3–1 pitch to left for two runs and a 4–2 lead, the biggest hit of the day. Brett lived up to his press clippings with a solo homer to left-center off Ron Davis in the seventh. Then Bob Watson dropped a routine throw from short, White singled for his third hit, and Willie Wilson scored the last two runs with a double to the centerfield warning track that Bobby Brown ran sideways on before deciding that the ball was over his head. Six of Kansas City's runs scored after two were out, and the Yankee outfield, as we've seen all year, did not distinguish itself.

Thursday, October 9. A.M. Tonight I will switch television stations. There is a battle going on for the New York audience between ABC, which has national rights to televise the Playoffs, and WPIX, which broadcast Yankee games locally during the year. If ABC had assigned Howard Cosell to the Yankee-Royal series my choice would be easy, but the network wisely has Howard, along with Keith Jackson and Don Drysdale, in Philadelphia, which gives him an almost captive audience in New York. In another smart move, ABC not only recruited the smooth-talking, good-looking underwear model, Jim Palmer, to help Al Michaels announce the Yankee-K.C. games, it rounded off the broadcasting team with the famous author of the hot-selling autobiography *Number One,* Billy Martin.

Billy's presence on the air creates a dilemma for the Yankee loyalist, as well as the Yankee-hater. It would normally be easy to scorn the interloping network heavies, who set obscure game times and delay innings for extra commercials, in favor of the White-Messer-Rizzuto troika that paid its dues and carried us this far. But whatever I may think of him, Billy is unquestionably one of the most popular Yankees, in or out of pinstripes. Just as there are many people who wish Richard Nixon were still President, there are an awful lot of New Yorkers who would give Howser's job back to Billy tomorrow if they had the chance. Those of us who are slightly more objective have to acknowledge that if anybody is in a position to contribute new insights on the Yankee players and management, it's Billy. And what about his views on the Royals, a team that Billy single-handedly psyched out of the Playoffs in '76 and '77? When the Royals led two games to one in '77 and scheduled ex-Yankee Larry Gura to start the fourth game, Martin said he would send a limousine to make sure Gura arrived at the park safely. According to Yankee reliever Doug Bird, who was then with Kansas City, "Maybe it wasn't so much a matter of intimidation, but Gura wanted to beat him bad and he tried too hard." Billy's most famous quote, however, was about Reggie and George—"One's a born liar and the other's convicted"—and everybody out here in TV-land would love to be listening in case Billy slips into honesty again.

While the addition of Martin will surely help ABC's ratings, you've got to wonder what it will do to his famous relationship with the Scooter. No one, repeat no one, stuck up for Billy Martin through his various misdeeds and hard times more steadfastly than Phil Rizzuto. At one point Rizzuto's job was even in jeopardy because he took Billy's side in the conflict with George Steinbrenner. Now, when the Yankee broadcasters are in a ratings fight with the rich boys from Sixth Avenue, who comes around to stick a mike in the Scooter's back? The radio ads this week have featured Rizzuto's appeal to fan loyalty: "Join WPIX, which has brought you the Yankee games for the last thirty years. . . . We know the Yankees and you know us." I'm coming back tonight, Phil. Just don't look for any loyalty—to anyone but number one—from Billy Martin.

Martin's presence would be a less blatant attempt to steal New York viewers from WPIX if he could speak grammatical English or was a candidate for an announcing career, like the man he succeeded as Yankee second baseman. Jerry Coleman was fired just last week as San Diego Padre manager with the comment, "We examined the needs of the Padre organization and concluded that Jerry would be more valuable to us in the broadcast booth." Coleman, coincidentally, is announcing the Playoffs in his own right, serving as sidekick to Cardinal announcer Jack Buck on CBS's radio broadcast from Philly, which is offered for the millions of discriminating fans who turn off the sound on Howard and the Big D. But Billy's first comment of the series-opening game, before he even realized that his mike was on, summed up his broadcasting savoir faire: "Is it all right if I wear my sunglasses?"

Once the game got going, Billy didn't make any horrible gaffes, but he didn't tell us much, either—and most disappointing, he had nothing bad to say about anybody. In his favor, he and Palmer never talked just to hear themselves speak, and they seldom got in the way of the play-by-play. At times, it actually sounded like a baseball game we were listening to, in comparison to the noise the other bunch made in Philadelphia.

I'll know I'm not missing anything tonight, however, when I rejoin the regular crew on WPIX. The only thing that might get me back to ABC is if my switch leads to a Yankee win. This series is too important for me to influence its outcome just because I would rather listen to Phil Rizzuto than Billy Martin.

Thursday, October 9. P.M. George Steinbrenner didn't have any trouble finding goats to pin the Yankees' first-game loss on. There was Bucky Dent, who veered away from the popup that scored the Royals' first two runs. There was Ron Guidry, who gave up four runs on four hits and four walks (one intentional) in three innings, although the two run-scoring hits were fluky at best. And there was George's favorite whipping boy, Reggie Jackson, who, like Bobby Brown, was o-for-4, except that Brown bats ninth. "You can't pitch for your pitcher and hit for your cleanup hitter," said George, meaning something, I'm sure. "If Reggie doesn't perform, we don't win." "The game always looks easy from up there," Dent replied.

But when the Yankees dropped the second game tonight, 3–2, George had to go a ways to find a culprit. This time the Yankees, unlike the Royals, played almost flawlessly in the field. Bobby Brown actually got a jump on a long drive to center by Hal McRae and turned it into an easy play. Reggie played Wilson's shot down the rightfield line very smoothly and held him to a triple. And Rudy May's pitching could not be faulted: he hung the collar on Brett and gave up only six hits and three walks in going the route. He had only one bad inning, the third, when Porter, White, Wilson and Washington stung four solid hits for all three Kansas City runs. As for the Royals' vaunted speed, Otis stole a base but Cerone threw out McRae. Wilson, on first twice, didn't even try.

No, in George's words, "My players didn't lose this one." Who did? Would you believe the third-base coach? Maybe George got the idea from watching the Phillies' sickening second-game loss to the Astros, when in the bottom of the ninth with the score tied, Bake McBride failed to score from second base on Lonnie Smith's looping single to rightfield. McBride held at third, which didn't seem fatal with one out; but when the next two batters couldn't hit a fair ball and the Astros scored four times in the tenth, all eyes went back to McBride's baserunning and Philadelphia's previously anonymous third-base coach, Lee Elia. Elia had held up his hands as McBride neared third, thinking that Houston's Terry Puhl had a chance to catch the ball on the fly. When it dropped, Elia waved McBride on with a seal-like gesture, but McBride had stopped to look at rightfield himself and couldn't get started again. Puhl made a strong throw home, and the only way McBride could have scored is if he had ignored from the start the possibility of being doubled off second, probably an unreasonable risk in that situation. But by running to third and then stopping, McBride got the worst of both options. And for his part, Elia ended up looking foolish on national TV.

As for the Yankees' third-base coach, Mike Ferraro, all he did was wave Willie Randolph around third, attempting to score him from first on Bob Watson's two-out double in the eighth, with Kansas City clinging to a narrow 3–2 lead. There's no way you stop Randolph on third in that situation. He's one of the Yankees' two fastest baserunners, and Wilson's throw from left was a rainbow headed over the cutoff man. The odds that Brett, the backup relay man, would make a perfect throw and that Porter would hold a ball arriving a split second before Randolph were far smaller than the chance that Oscar Gamble (who would be up after they walked Reggie) would, with two outs, get Randolph home from third. I feel this way, the TV announcers agree, so does Howser, so does Randolph. But we don't sign the paychecks. "I was dead against it when it happened. We got Reggie and Oscar sitting there," grumbled the boss. Then referring to Ferraro, "He's been doing it all year." Apparently, George got off the crowded elevator he was talking to without elaborating on what the "it" is, and the press covering the Yankees can't recall any previous controversy involving Ferraro. As for third-base coaching in general, Billy Martin was quoted as saying, "It's the toughest job in baseball," as I suspect Clete Boyer learned from Billy the hard way this year.

With Reggie not hitting any home runs, George has dominated the Yankee news so far this Playoff. No doubt taking full credit for New York's remarkable September after he pasted the troops for blowing the Baltimore series in August, George believes his barbs here will produce similar results against the Royals. "He wants me to read that in the papers and get riled up," Reggie observed sagely after the first game, and sure enough, the big fellow went 2-for-4 tonight. The question now is, have you ever seen a riled-up third-base coach, and what's he supposed to do if he is?

Friday, October 10. 9:30 P.M. There's no score in the fourth inning of Playoff game number three, and the rain has brought out the Yankee Stadium ground crew to unroll the tarpaulin. For the first time this year I am faced with a dreaded dilemma: I want the Yankees to lose, but I don't want their season to end, and if they lose tonight, that's all she wrote. I especially don't want it to end with a quiet, low-scoring game like the sleeper this afternoon between the Phils and Astros, and with Tommy John pitching that's the prospect for tonight. I'd at least like to see the series go till tomorrow, when Luis Tiant and Rich Gale are scheduled to start, two righthanders who should bring out the best in both teams' lefthanded attacks. Coincidentally, they were the starters of the game I attended in Kansas City this July, which would provide a handy book-end for this year's diary.

The Astros this afternoon beat the Phillies 1–0 in eleven innings to take a 2–1 lead in the Playoff series, but they lost centerfielder Cesar Cedeno for the year in the effort. That gives me two more reasons I don't want New York to get past the Royals. A Kansas City–Houston series, with two speedy Astroturf teams in the World Series for the first times in those cities' history, would be full of new faces, surprises and fun. But more important, I seriously doubt that the Astros, in the circumstances, could beat the Yankees. And more important to me than when the season ends, is how it ends.

Friday, October 10. 11:00 P.M. The Yankees just took the lead, 2–1, on an amazingly ill-advised throw over third by hitting hero Frank White that all-around hero George Brett ended up kicking into the Royal dugout. Not only did Jackson, who had doubled, score the tying run, but Gamble, who hit the ground ball up the middle that White fielded, wound up at third. The Kansas City infield had to play in, and Washington had no chance on Cerone's soft liner over short. For the first time all series, the Royals are in Goose country, the fans know it, and momentum has shifted. If the Yankees can hold this lead, the pressure tomorrow, I am afraid, will be on the Royals, not the Yanks.

Friday, October 10. 11:15 P.M. WPIX opened the seventh inning with this statistic on the screen: the Yankees won 77 of 79 games in which they took a lead into the seventh inning. I'm not sure I believe that, but the general point is well taken. When Willie Wilson hit a fly into the rightfield corner with two outs that Reggie played gingerly, as usual, I was annoyed to see him stop at second base. Because I knew, and Wilson should have known, that we would now be seeing the Goose. Sure, Wilson could score from second as easily as third on a base hit to the outfield, but there are more wild pitches and passed balls than base hits when the Goose comes on. My point was made, I thought, when the next batter, U. L. Washington, beat out a slow grounder to second. Instead of the game's being tied, we needed yet another hit, and the next batter had gone hitless in his last seven at-bats. His name, however, was George Brett. Gossage kicked and delivered a 98-mph fastball. Brett was out in front of it and parked it in the upper deck of the rightfield stands. Kansas City now leads, 4–2. And the Yankees' record on holding seventh-inning leads is in danger of plummeting to 77–3.

Friday, October 10. 11:55 P.M. The game is over, the Yankee season is over, the pennant can now be raised in Kansas City. The Royals won tonight, 4–2, in a contest, finally, that rose to the level of championship play I've been waiting for all year. And in the tense final three innings, the entire Yankee season passed before my eyes.

The New York Yankees won 103 games this year—the most in the majors, and the most by a Yankee team since 1963—but *the* baseball story in the American League in 1980 was not the Yankees, it was George Brett's run at hitting .400. Tonight the Yankees were eclipsed by Brett one last time.

The Yankees' most valuable player in 1980, the one most responsible for that incredible late-inning success record, was Goose Gossage. How fitting that tonight's game came down to a confrontation between the Yankees' MVP and the Royals' MVP, a man who spoke of Gossage in awe during the rain delay earlier in the evening. When the Goose was beaten, the Yankees were, too.

Bob Watson was the Yanks' steadiest hitter all year. I had predicted that he would never seem like a real Yankee, and he didn't: there was no flamboyance, there were no complaints, there was even an incongruous stab at team spirit when he called a players-only meeting during the summer slump. Watson alone didn't know that the season was over after Brett's home run, and he tripled to lead off the eighth inning, his third hit of the game.

Next up was Reggie Jackson, the putative MVP candidate, about whose season an entire book could be written, and probably will be. The Orioles destroyed Reggie's rhythm by pitching around him in August, and I didn't see him swing with confidence thereafter. He had a five-day flurry that brought his average up to .300 and helped the Yankees clinch the division, but most of those games weren't on TV; when he opened the Playoffs with a weak 0-for-4 against Gura he was back where he was in September. With Watson on third, Reggie, the Big Man, had to bring him home, but with the count 2–2 Reggie took two pitches that I would have called strikes but the umpire gave him for a walk. How far had Reggie fallen since the drama of 1977?

How far was answered two batters later, when with the bases loaded and no outs Rick Cerone hit another liner to shortstop. Only this one was caught, easily, and Reggie was doubled off second base, very easily. It was a monumental baserunning blunder by an ultimately one-dimensional baseball player.

As for Cerone, he got the Yankees' only RBI on the day and almost had two more. His game and his series were just like his year: unspectacular but solid. He did his job and he had fun.

That left it up to Jim Spencer, relegated as usual to a pinch-hitting role. He felt underutilized all year, and this was his first time at bat in the Playoffs. But all year he hit only .236, and this time he hit a grounder to second that would have been a doubleplay if Reggie hadn't already taken care of that.

Spencer had batted for Lou Piniella, who started the Playoffs with a home run, then never got another hit. For Lou, being lifted here was the season's final frustration.

Tommy Underwood pitched the eighth and ninth innings for New York, the kind of thankless task that Underwood performed all year. He was little noticed or appreciated, but he pitched more innings for Howser this year than anyone on the staff except Guidry and John. And with the help of a pick-off of Otis, he retired all six Royals he faced.

Joe Lefebvre went out to leftfield in the ninth, after Spencer pinch-hit for Piniella, a token reminder of the almost-forgotten rookie-development program. After being sent to the minors in July, Lefebvre never regained the hitting stroke that had made him a phee-nom in May. Unlike Dennis Werth he never got the clutch hit, and unlike Werth he was never accepted by the veterans, who seemed to resent his clean-cut hustle.

In the ninth the Yankees' dugout was quiet. No one led any cheers. The network announcers commented on this, per-haps expecting to see some of the rah-rah spirit the Astros were winning with in the National League. But the dugout scene accurately reflected these Yankees—a collection of individuals who win, when they win, on professionalism, not inspiration.

This time the Yankees went down meekly, the mark of a defeated club—or at least a club that is not used to having a seventh-inning lead taken away from it. Nettles hit an easy fly to Otis. Bobby Brown, 0-for-10, hit an easy fly to Wilson.

Willie Randolph ended up leading the league in bases on balls. By the end of the year I understood a little better how he did it. First, he has a good eye; second, he looks for walks. He crouches at the plate and ducks under chest-high pitches. If they're on the inside corner he twists away. With two out in the ninth he argued the call on the first pitch. He was looking for one more walk, to bring the tying run to the plate. He worked the count to 3-2. Quisenberry's pitch went up and down, but it stayed on the inside corner of the plate. Randolph started to first. Umpire Larry McCoy's right arm went high in the air. The walk king had gone to the well once too often.

In the on-deck circle was pinch hitter Bobby Murcer, ready to bat for Bucky Dent. Murcer must hold the modern record for most years played with the New York Yankees without ever being in a World Series. Add one more year to that record. And for perhaps the last time ever, Bobby Murcer lost another chance to make them forget Mickey Mantle.

Saturday, October 11. The newspapers today are covering the NBA season, which opened yesterday, and the NHL season, which opened the day before. The baseball season still has two weeks to go, in what I hope will be a good World Series between the Royals and the Astros, two deserving teams whose time has come and whose new blood is appreciated—by me, if not by NBC. And if somehow the Phils can come back, I would certainly not begrudge a World Series victory for the only one of the original 16 teams that can still say it has never won a World Series.

But with the Yankees' loss to the Royals, the 1980 baseball season in New York is over. There are some award announcements to come, but they shouldn't involve the Yankees this year: Steve Stone is the Cy Young winner and George Brett the MVP, without any doubt in my mind. The newspaper writers whom I have relied on all year will have some final thoughts, but when one team loses eight of twelve regular-season games then three straight Playoff games to another team, the postmortems need not look too far for a cause of death.

When Frank Messer and Bill White shook hands and wound up the TV broadcast, while Fran and the Scooter were saying so long on the radio, I, too, took my leave from this 1980 season. I got what I wanted, I guess, a Yankee defeat at the hands of the Royals—repayment, if somewhat late and inevitably incomplete, for the Yankee Playoff wins in 1976, 1977 and 1978. But after the first moment of "pure elation" (Quisenberry's reaction to Brett's homer), I sank into thoughts of nostalgia for the season and was overcome by a feeling of emptiness, for the baseball-less winter ahead.

On last night's postgame show, the briefest one of the year, Messer observed that Steinbrenner will undoubtedly start making some changes. That picked my spirits up. Will George go after Winfield? Will Howser be back? What will happen to Murcer and Piniella? What about Reggie's contract? What about the Yankees' 40-year-old pitching staff? Their aging third basemen? Will Steinbrenner ever want to see Spencer and Soderholm again? Will the rookies, and the players I scouted in Nashville, get a chance? What about . . .

But that is next year. This year's diary is closed.